FUNDING
the FUTURE

Bob Craves
with Tony Dirksen

Funding the Future

Practical Strategies for Scholarship Development

2006 © Bob Craves

All rights reserved.

Cover design by Bob Craves and Beth Farrell

Text design and layout by Beth Farrell

Featuring photographs by Mel Curtis

www.melcurtis.com

Sea Script Company

Seattle, Washington

ISBN: 0-9672186-2-4 (softcover)

Library of Congress Card Catalogue No.: 2006922000

First Printing February 2006

www.nationaledfoundation.org

NATIONAL EDUCATION FOUNDATION

SEA   SCRIPT   COMPANY
1800 westlake ave n. ste 205 seattle wa 98109
tel 206.748.0345 fax 206.748.0343
info@seascriptcompany.com

WHAT'S WRONG WITH THIS PICTURE? Visualize 60,000 seniors graduating from high school in their colorful robes. But 28,000 never go to college. Of those who do, only half earn their baccalaureate degree in six years. What this means is that 44,000 young adults enter the 21st century workforce with no college degree and very little post-secondary education—year after year after year.

This is a tragic waste. Especially when you realize that at least 6,000 of those students that didn't go to college or didn't finish their degree could have been successful in a baccalaureate program, but didn't attend or finish simply because they didn't have the money.

The Washington Education Foundation was founded in 2000 to provide college scholarships and mentoring to low-income, high potential students. Today thanks to hundreds of generous benefactors, 3,100 of these students are in school working to earn their bachelor's degrees and begin their adult lives with the solid grounding of a quality education.

TABLE OF CONTENTS

Our Heroes

FOREWORD

EDUCATION IS THE GREAT EQUALIZER IN OUR SOCIETY. Regardless of your income level, your gender, or your ethnic origin, education puts everyone on a level playing field and enables all people to take advantage of the incredible opportunities in America.

Education has also been one of the great attractions of America for wave after wave of immigrants. College education is part of the American dream. It was part of my family's dream as well, when they came to America from China.

In my home, education and learning were part of the ethic of our family. Our parents always said, "You're going to go to college." We didn't know, however, how we were going to pay for it.

Mom and Dad worked seven days a week, 14 hours a day, running a grocery store. They worked hard to take care of our family. The store never closed, whether it was Christmas or New Year's.

Even while they were working, whether in the back room of the store or back at home in the kitchen, Mom and Dad would do things like write out math tables—"2 plus 2 equals 4 and 5 times 5 equals 25" and the like—while they were cooking at home or just running the business.

We've always had a thirst for education in my family. All the children in our family went to college. Financial aid made all the difference in the world. It was part-time jobs and loans plus the modest contribution from the family (as much as they could help out), along with scholarships and financial aid that made it possible for me, as well as my sisters and brother, to earn our degrees.

Our parents always had high expectations that we would become engineers, doctors, or professionals. A sister right behind me is an accountant; my younger brother is a software engineer; another sister was an auditor at Nordstrom. As you can imagine, our parents are incredibly proud.

It's because of these personal experiences that I've been a big believer in scholarships. I know how critically important they are, and how important education is. Without scholarships, so many people would not be able to attend our universities, especially since tuition plus room-and-board costs are getting so much more expensive these days.

Early in my administration as Governor, we established the 2020 Commission on the Future of Post-Secondary Education to develop a roadmap to the future for our colleges and universities so that we could figure out where we needed to be 20 to 30 years from now. As a state, we needed to start moving in that direction, making sure that all of our actions were consistent with those desired goals.

We kept hearing of the impending demand for college education and the need to increase enrollments. We needed to have a systematic way of supporting higher education and getting our colleges and universities to both increase their enrollments and improve the quality of their education. I felt that we just couldn't wait until the very last minute years from now before we embarked on the necessary actions.

As co-chair of the 2020 Commission, Bob Craves was instrumental in helping to establish that roadmap for the future. But he stepped above and beyond the call of duty by taking the 15th recommendation of the Commission—to establish an independent, non-profit organization to build and sustain public understanding of the need for higher levels of educational attainment and lifelong learning—and established the Washington Education Foundation.

The Washington Education Foundation is a shining example of what's needed in America. It provides comprehensive scholarship and financial aid opportunities, not just in terms of dollars, but also in terms of services—from meeting the housing needs of students to providing mentoring, guidance, and other support while students are in college. For a lot of young people going off to college, it's overwhelming—they're entering a strange and different community, a totally different atmosphere. So it's not enough just to provide the financial help, we also need to assist with guidance and reassurance along the way, which the Washington Education Foundation does so well.

As Governor, I worked directly with the Foundation to create the Governor's Scholarship, which provides support to foster children entering college. There are certainly many changes we need to explore in our foster-care system but at the same time, for those who are currently going through it, we need to give them hope. A lot of foster children lose whatever government or foster-care support they have when they turn 18 or graduate from high school. The result is that only a small percentage ever go on to college. And of those that do, many drop out because they're trying to work full-time and carry a full load—they just can't do both.

Our approach with the Governor's Scholarship was that we wanted to make sure these foster children had the financial means to get all the way through their college education if they so desired. We don't want kids to be enrolled in college and then suddenly become stranded, so we provide four full years of support. The program has been a big success, and every year we are raising more money than the previous year. When you hear the stories of the kids, it's so heartbreaking and inspiring. I remember one girl who said her mom and dad died of drug overdoses, and she got bounced around from family to family. She realized that her ticket to a brighter future would be through education and a good-paying job. She applied herself, received a Governor's Scholarship, and graduated from college in 2006. We're so proud of her, but she is really typical of a lot of these recipients with their tough backgrounds and the struggles they've faced as well as the incredible successes they've demonstrated.

Another important program from my tenure as Governor is the Washington Promise Scholarship, which is built on the premise that we should be telling children and their parents that if they do well in high school, there will be a scholarship waiting for them when they graduate. By making it a program of the state, we can reinforce the message—through counselors, parents, grandparents, and community leaders—that there will be a scholarship waiting for children who do well in school.

If we want to break down the divides between the haves and the have-nots, it's going to be through education. But because college education is so expensive, we've got to address the economics—and that means financial aid. States have a myriad of approaches on how they do that but government can't, and won't, do it all. Government can't fix everything for everybody.

That's where organizations like the Washington Education Foundation stand out. They're targeting kids early, and they're providing mentoring to those students with the promise that if they do well, there will be financial help to attend college. And that's a message that has to be conveyed at an early age, and conveyed also to parents. If parents believe that even though *they* didn't have the means to go to college, their kids can, those parents are reinforced when they urge their kids to study and do well. Otherwise, there's no hope.

The availability of education, made possible and fueled by scholarships such as the GI Bill that Bob describes in this book, enabled America to emerge as the dominant economy in the world and as the land of innovation and creativity that has transformed the rest of the world—in medicine, engineering, technology, science or the exploration of outer space. These accomplishments were possible because of a highly educated work force.

If we want our kids here in Washington to have a chance at these jobs of the future in this global high-tech 21st-century economy, we need to make sure we have a high-quality education system, and we need to make sure our young people can take advantage of those opportunities. Otherwise, companies are going to hire people from some other state or country, and *our* children will be left behind. Which means that all of us will have to support these young future adults as they mature through human services and the criminal justice system—a tragic waste.

As a nation and as a state, we have so much to celebrate, so many accomplishments that were made possible thanks to our highly educated work force. As we look forward to the next 20 years, having organizations such as the Washington Education Foundation in other states will help—through their innovative support of education— make America an even better nation than it is today.

—Gary Locke
Former Governor
Washington State

Acknowledgements

To my wife Gerri—thanks, not only for accepting my decision to leave a very interesting and lucrative career to try to help thousands of young college students complete their baccalaureate degrees, but also for everything she has done to help the Washington Education Foundation get off the ground.

Thanks also to Ann Ramsay-Jenkins, who believed in the dream from day one and who continues to bring happiness to everyone who works with us.

And to the wonderful staff of the Washington Education Foundation, particularly those first members who admittedly took a big chance when they jumped on board: Steve Thorndill, who oversaw all the scholarship and support programs; Tanguy Martin, who put together our systems; and Kelly Fagan, who pulled all the details together.

A special thanks as well to all my friends at Costco—especially Jim Sinegal, Jeff Brotman, Dick DiCerchio, Craig Jelinek, Joel Benoliel, and Art Jackson—not only for being passionate about helping low-income children go to college and helping us get the Foundation off the ground, but also for setting up the annual Costco Scholarship Fund Breakfast to help hundreds of kids go to college.

Though they never ask for thanks, a very special thank-you to the Bill and Melinda Gates Foundation and especially to Bill Gates Sr., Patty Stonesifer, Tom Vander Ark, and Dr. Deborah Wilds for believing in the project and contributing not only money and great insight, but also for helping direct our efforts.

Thanks to Governors Christine Gregoire and Gary Locke; Senators Lisa Brown, Rosemary McAullife, and Margarita Prentice; Speaker Frank Chopp; and Representatives Phyllis Gutierrez Kennedy,

Dave Quall, Ross Hunter, and Helen Sommers for all they did to help us from the earliest days of the Foundation, particularly as we established the Hometown Mentoring Program and the Governor's Cup for Scholarships for Foster Youth.

Thanks to the Washington State Higher Education Board, especially former Executive Director Marc Gaspard and Dr. James Sulton.

I would also like to thank Senator Patty Murray for helping us fund the National Education Foundation, and Senator Maria Cantwell, Congressmen Jay Inslee, Dave Reichert, and Congresswoman Cathy McMorris for helping us fund the Leadership 1000 Scholarship Program.

Thanks are also due to Ted Baseler at Château Ste. Michelle for hosting an annual dinner concert at the Château to raise money for scholarships.

Thanks to my Board of Directors: Joe Gaffney, Tricia Raikes, Sister Kathleen Ross, Fred Campbell, Sam Smith, Lonny Suko, Jerry Lee, and Merilee Frets, along with Governor Gary Locke, Gerri, Deborah and Ann, and our original board member, Jack Creighton.

Thanks to Tony Dirksen who did most of the work producing this book. And thanks to Larry Wright and Victoria Nelson for helping finish the book.

Finally, thanks to my daughter Stacie who became my real inspiration to help these kids. Watching her dedicate many years of her young life to earning her Doctorate in Clinical Psychology convinced me that there are many other less fortunate students that we could help.

Together with all of you, and future participants, we hope to make it possible to support, not only the thousands of students a year who need our help in Washington, but the tens of thousands more across the country who could benefit from what have found is an exciting new way to think about scholarship programs.

—Bob Craves
Chairman, President and CEO
National Education Foundation

PREFACE

THIS IS A STORY IN PROGRESS. This is a story about how a growing number of people concerned about the future of business and the future of education have come together to help a special group of kids: *the thousands of students who wouldn't be able to attend a four-year college without their help.* These are students with the brains, the grades, and certainly the drive that demonstrates they can succeed. They're students with the potential to serve as active and productive participants in the workforce of the 21st century, but without the financial and other resources required to get to college all by themselves.

For many of them, that means a lifetime of substandard jobs and wages, along with the inability to make a full contribution to our nation's economy.

These are the children each year that are not adequately served or supported by existing government and scholarship programs. Obviously, the personal impact on their lives is enormous. But the consequences of these young people not attending college actually affects all our students, even those who *can* afford to pay, because it can create universities that are isolated and don't reflect the realities of society at large.

We felt we could do better, which is why—working with people from different professions and with a broad range of financial capabilities—we created the Washington Education Foundation in 2000. Our goal? To put together a 20-year plan to deliver support to those students who are going to create the future.

We are nearing the quarter point in our 20-year journey, which makes this an appropriate time to look back over what we've accomplished, and look forward to what we still have to do.

This is a job that, in a sense, won't ever be finished, since new students arrive every year. Twenty years is really just a start!

Furthermore, these opportunities and needs are not unique to the state of Washington. That's why we hope this book will be of use to leaders in other states as they set out to put together their own scholarship programs.

While these efforts may have started in Seattle, they've now begun to sweep the nation, as other people in many other places start to build on our model, our experience, and our expertise.

We founded the National Education Foundation so that we could share our experience and our tools with the people across the country who are setting out to do the same sorts of things that we have accomplished in the state of Washington.

As advocates for education, we are increasingly raising post-secondary education issues to the national level, and representing the needs of students, educators, and other foundations that share our vision and our charter.

Through the National Education Foundation, we're able to offer our blueprint for success to these other states and foundations so that they can take our proven tools and, where appropriate, customize them to meet the particular needs of their local regions and individual scholarship programs.

Admittedly, we can't use a cookie-cutter approach. Not everything that worked in Washington will work exactly the same way everywhere else. Not every scholarship program has (or should have) the same requirements or parameters. For example, many of our scholarship efforts in Washington state were originally driven by social justice issues, which resulted from the passage of state Initiative 200 in 1998. While this unfortunate initiative prevented our state universities from offering scholarships in order to promote cultural and racial diversity on their campuses, it could not prohibit private companies and scholarship organizations from pinpointing their donations to these underrepresented groups. I might mention that people from both sides of the political spectrum shared disappointment with the implementation of Initiative 200. Not only is it important for minority students to participate in public higher education, it is incredibly important for the student body as a whole to be diverse to reflect the diversity of the real world.

Other states, more fortunate than ours, have not faced the particular type of challenge of an Initiative 200 to their existing programs. Instead, they may be in a position to bring their focus right away on the same sorts of directions that have become

Education is not preparation for life; education is life itself. -John Dewey

increasingly essential at the Washington Education Foundation: to develop the workforce of the 21st century—by supporting high-potential, low-income students who otherwise would not be in a position to participate fully in and contribute to that workforce.

We firmly believe that if we can help more and more young people to earn their four-year degrees, we'll all benefit as these students advance into careers in science, industry, and education. Their success in turn can benefit the overall economy, and will ultimately pay off for future generations of students as well.

At the Washington Education Foundation, there were a lot of things we were able to do right, but there have also been more than a few lessons we've had to learn along the way, lessons that we have taken to heart and shared with foundations in other states through our National Education Foundation efforts. We hope both will prove useful to you.

Ultimately, our goal is simple: to help students in need succeed. That's vitally important to the students, but the impact goes much farther. When we help young people rise above what is too often their fate—a lifetime of minimum-wage jobs—we make it possible instead for them to participate in the new economy.

The investment we make in these students today will produce large returns that can benefit all of us in the future.

WASHINGTON EDUCATION FOUNDATION: MISSION AND APPROACH

MISSION STATEMENT

The Washington Education Foundation provides college scholarships and mentoring to low-income, high-potential students.

ADVOCACY/SOCIAL CHANGE

The Washington Education Foundation seeks to reduce barriers that low-income students face across the entire educational system 1) by demonstrating that existing solutions are available in high schools and colleges, and 2) by advocating for educational reform on a local, state and national level.

SCHOLARSHIPS

The Washington Education Foundation helps bridge the gap between what students and their families can afford and what a quality education costs.

Working closely with a variety of companies and foundations, the Washington Education Foundation supports a wide range of scholarship programs. Because of the established working relationships between our staff and many of the leading educators, benefactors and volunteers throughout the state, we're able to distribute funds efficiently in a way that most effectively supports students and contributes to their success throughout their college experience.

SUPPORT SERVICES

In addition to scholarship assistance, the Washington Education Foundation offers mentoring and college planning support. Our services range from advice on the college admissions and financial aid process to guidance on year-round housing, academic assistance and health insurance. Our goal is to provide students with as much resource information as possible to help them feel comfortable navigating their way through the college experience and thereby to promote their academic success.

MENTORING

The Washington Education Foundation believes mentoring is the ideal way to transition many young people from high school through their first years of college. A caring, adult mentor who understands the college experience is critical to helping these students see college as attainable—especially those who are the first in their family to attend.

OUR STORY SO FAR

As the Washington Education Foundation completes its fifth year, we're able to celebrate the fact that a growing number of students have received their bachelor's degrees through our scholarship programs.

We're extremely proud of these students. We know that it is only the beginning for them as they initiate careers that will span government, business, medicine, law, education, engineering and many other fields.

These students—many of whom would have otherwise been left behind—are joining the workforce of the 21st century, and in many cases also making major contributions to their home communities. Several of them, for example, have returned to their own high schools and encouraged other graduating students to apply for scholarships.

What's more, many of these students have given us outstanding feedback on how we can best shape and evolve our programs.

We're making changes every day in how we do things—changes and refinements that will allow us to better serve the needs of our students and of our communities.

A lot of what we do as a Foundation is, quite simply, to spread the word about the many educational needs in our community, and about the many opportunities that will open up if we address those needs.

Sometimes we're talking with students—at both the high-school and the university level—hoping to guide them to make good educational choices while also listening attentively to understand clearly the challenges they're facing in their young lives and how we can do things better to help them.

Other times, we're talking with educators, people that I've come to recognize have a deep abiding commitment to serving the public good, and who have dedicated their lives to bringing out excellence in other people. I see this dedication in every level of educator I've encountered so far, from university presidents to kindergarten teachers. The people who have committed their lives to education are a very special group of individuals. I admire them greatly and consider it an honor to be working with them.

Often, we're talking to senior executives in corporations as well as to private individuals, in one-on-one settings, to help them understand the needs and to encourage their donations. An interesting point here—I've been amazed at how often these individuals come to us, already committed to the cause, just looking for an organization with strong ties into the scholarship world. Most people, I'm convinced, want to be a part of making good things happen.

Corporations and individuals considering donations typically, and justifiably, want to ensure that their donations are put to good use. Since I came from the business community, I both respect and understand that perspective. That's why, as we've built the Washington Education Foundation, we've always tried to run it according to sound business principles. And we're fortunate enough to have hired some of the best people I've ever worked with, people who share our commitment to the cause of education and who are highly focused on getting the most dollars to students in the most efficient and most intelligent way possible.

Sometimes our conversations are with other foundations, to explain what we have accomplished in Washington state and how we did it. We know that the needs we identified and are living with in Washington are reflected in many other places around the country. If we can create an opportunity for discussion that helps these thousands upon thousands of students in other states get an education, we'll see the value of our work multiplied many times over.

On a regular basis, we're also talking with our government representatives. On occasion we've been requested to appear at government hearings at the local, state and federal levels. We relish these opportunities because we firmly believe in the idea of a public/private partnership for education.

We believe that government has an important role in leading the charge in improving the overall educational environment.

We recognize, however, that governments face challenges as well, not only in terms of addressing many of the major issues facing our society, but doing it at a time when many government entities are struggling just to make ends meet, unable to expand their distribution of money and other resources.

That's why we focus our scholarship programs on the idea of the "last dollar in"—another concept we'll discuss in detail in a later chapter. Our belief is that we can serve students' needs best not by replacing government and other public grants, but by augmenting them—closing the gap by providing the remainder of the funds that are truly necessary for students to attend college.

And that's also where the private part of the "partnership" comes in. By working closely with our government, and by serving as one vocal representative for educational needs, we feel we can have a positive influence on where our country is headed. And by backing up our voice with actual scholarships, we're literally putting our money where our mouth is.

We all share a concern for improving education. At the same

time, society has many needs competing for the limited resources to solve them. Our job is to focus our efforts on baccalaureate education as one essential part of shaping the future.

And it's a future that's already here. When we talk about creating the workforce of the 21st century, it's important for all of us to remember that we've already arrived. The decisions we make today, in the early part of this century, will have an enormous influence on the next several generations.

We'll be judged by our actions, both now and in the future.

By our actions, we're making decisions right now that will affect whether our country will continue the greatest period of business and scientific growth in its history—a period of growth in the 1990s that was driven in large part by increased gains in education.

By our actions, we'll determine whether our multi-cultural society will come together and create a stronger country in which people mutually respect each other, or a fragmented contentious battleground.

None of us wants that to happen. That's why, at the Washington Education Foundation, we've set out to light our one candle in the proverbial darkness in order to make this corner of the country a better place to live and work, a better place to raise families and create dreams for the future.

But we recognize that we're just at the starting gate. The possibilities of what we can accomplish are unlimited, but our time is not. So we're directing our efforts in ways that we believe will do the most good for the most people, by creating scholarship programs that seek to dramatically grow the number of people in a variety of professions—including doctors and lawyers, scientists, community workers and businesspeople, as well as math and science teachers and many other professionals who can actively participate in the excitement of the century ahead.

Looking forward, we've established some aggressive goals for the next ten years—initiating, in a sense, another ten-year journey.

By the end of that period, we expect the impact of our efforts to increase the total number of bachelor's degrees granted in Washington state by more than 10,000 students.

We also know that our graduates will be a positive force for change as they help their younger siblings, cousins, friends and the next generation of students to achieve to their maximum potential.

Sometimes it's said, "the journey is the reward." We believe there are many rewards we receive right now through our work with students—especially the excitement we see in students heading to four-year universities instead of dead-end jobs.

Every year, hundreds of our scholarship recipients attend a multi-day event in which they learn about the college application process and the Washington state colleges available to them. On the final day we put on a musical slide show in which those colleges are highlighted. I'm always touched when I hear these students cheer as their chosen schools appear on the screen, especially when I realize that most of them wouldn't be attending college at all without the help of the Foundation. They're able for the first time to live their dreams at the many fine private and public universities in our state.

These are the kinds of rewards we all relish, right now.

But the real rewards will come later—when these students complete their journey through college, and head off into the journey of adult life.

In 2005, the scholarship recipients of the Washington Education Foundation graduated from the following four-year colleges:

The Catholic University of America
Central Washington University
Cornish College
Eastern Washington University
Evergreen State University
Gonzaga University
Northwest College

Pacific Lutheran University
Saint Martin's College
Seattle University
University of Puget Sound
University of Washington—Bothell
University of Washington—Seattle
Washington State University—Pullman
Washington State University—Vancouver
Western Washington University
Whitman College
Whitworth College

WASHINGTON EDUCATION FOUNDATION: ACCOMPLISHMENTS SO FAR

Four Year Scholarships
(cumulative)

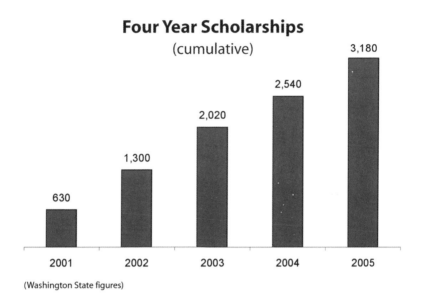

(Washington State figures)

Scholarship Dollars Disbursed
(in millions, cumulative)

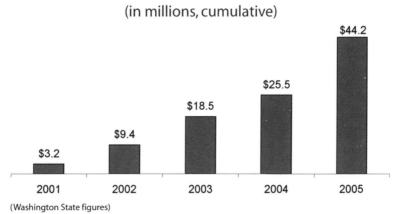

(Washington State figures)

FUNDING THE FUTURE
PRACTICAL STRATEGIES FOR SCHOLARSHIP DEVELOPMENT

1

DARE TO DREAM

WHEN WE BEGAN THE WASHINGTON EDUCATION FOUNDATION, we didn't set out right away to create any particular kind of organization. Instead, it was really a spin-off of Governor Locke's 2020 Commission on the Future of Post-Secondary Education, originally convened in 1998, which made 15 recommendations for what we needed to do to set up a more successful higher-education structure in the state of Washington to get us to the year 2020.

Education beyond high school is, in our view, increasingly essential as a way out of joblessness and poverty. Higher education not only broadens one's view of the world, it also increases productivity and creates a well-educated citizenry that can contribute to the vitality of communities, the state of Washington and the nation.

Ultimately, education is the ticket to a comfortable and stable income and challenging work. And giving kids the chance to punch that ticket will benefit not only the students themselves, but all of us as we enter this new century.

Increasingly, employers in Washington state tell us that they find it difficult to find educated workers. And locating out-of-state candidates is getting more difficult as well, forcing many of our own employers to look overseas, and even to transfer some of their operations there.

Yet for many children who live in low-income homes, post-secondary education is simply not considered possible. In fact, disparities in educational attainment between young adults from families with low incomes and kids from high-income families are large, pervasive and persistent—and the gap is growing larger every year.

Certainly, there are major issues of social justice here, which initially drove many of us to pay serious attention to these problems. But it's not just a question of whether our society and educational systems are fair. Instead, it comes down to a very practical issue: Can we, as a society, afford to lose the talents of these potentially successful students?

As it stands, the skills required for the jobs of the 21st century are more demanding than they were in the past. But our country's workforce requirements simply are not being met. Think about it. In 1986, when the graduating class of 1999 entered kindergarten in the state of Washington, there were upwards of 90,000 enthusiastic and wide-eyed children starting school. These were kids full of dreams and excitement about learning and school.

Of these, only 60,000 finished high school. Only 32,000 went to college. And only a fraction of those children received their diplomas.

We wanted to play a part in changing that. So the Governor's Commission put together a series of recommendations that were designed to ensure that our educational system could provide genuine support to the broad range of students in Washington state who needed it. (You can find the complete list of recommendations on page 149.)

As is true of a lot of commissions, some people said our report was going to end up as shelf art or, even worse, a doorstop. As the Chair of the Higher Education Coordinating Board for the state, I didn't want that to happen—mainly for the sake of the students, but also because of the energy that had been committed to the project by the dedicated commissioners, who included people like former Governor Dan Evans, Microsoft General Counsel Bill Neukom, Phyllis Campbell, the former President of US Bank and now the CEO of the Seattle Foundation, and most importantly, my co-chair Jack Creighton, the former CEO of Weyerhaeuser and United Airlines and a founding board member of the Washington Education Foundation.

The Commission produced 15 recommendations covering a broad range of long-term considerations for education in our state. The 15th recommendation of the Commission was that there needed to be a statewide advocacy group that would work diligently to open up access and, in the process, produce a lot more college graduates.

It could be built around, we thought, a sort of public/private partnership that would allow individuals to contribute, with the cooperation and blessing of the government.

As noted in the report:

> "An independent, non-profit organization is needed to educate community and business leaders and the public about the importance of post-secondary education; to advocate for expansion and improvement of the system; and to facilitate state government and the post-secondary education system accountability for meeting the needs of Washington learners. . .[The organization should be] composed of business, labor, education, and community leaders, should be created to promote continuous improvement of this state's post-secondary education system, and to build public support for it."

So I decided to take on the 15th recommendation and get things rolling by inviting a lot of people—legislators, college presidents and concerned citizens—to attend our first meeting. We held the meeting at Costco and served those famous "100-pound" Costco muffins with coffee.

There were some critical facts we shared with this audience. For example, the number of students that qualify for free or reduced-price lunches represents one measure of how well their families are doing economically. Since 1998, the numbers have grown dramatically worse in the state of Washington (which reflects patterns in the rest of the country as well).

% of Students on Free and Reduced Lunch in Public Schools

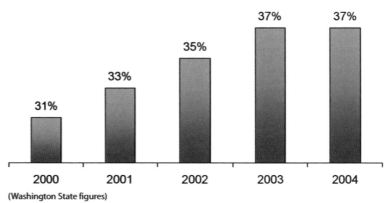

(Washington State figures)

These numbers are startling. More than one out of every three kids at the K–12 level depend on this program to get a decent meal! That's over 300,000 students every day in 2000. In 2004 it escalated to 375,000 students.

That's an early picture of what would later translate into some alarming data about our students. After reviewing census data we discovered that Washington state ranked 33rd among all states in the percentage of adults earning bachelor's degrees. And even worse, Washington ranked 46th in upper-division participation by junior and senior students.

Students have had to pay an ever-increasing percentage of their college tuition as costs went up and support went down.

Clearly, all the trends were headed in the wrong direction.

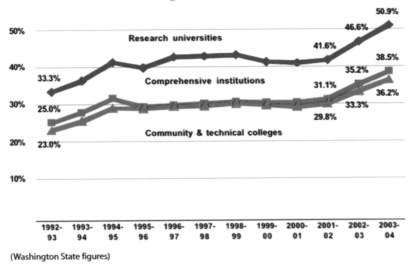

Rising Tuition Costs

Research universities

Comprehensive institutions

Community & technical colleges

50.9%
46.6%
41.6%
38.5%
35.2%
33.3%
31.1%
36.2%
33.3%
29.8%
25.0%
23.0%

| 1992-93 | 1993-94 | 1994-95 | 1995-96 | 1996-97 | 1997-98 | 1998-99 | 1999-00 | 2000-01 | 2001-02 | 2002-03 | 2003-04 |

(Washington State figures)

As we presented this information, everyone backed the idea of supporting our educational needs, but to be honest, hardly anybody was really ready to take the ball and run with it. They agreed this was a very good idea, and then they left.

Fewer people attended the second meeting. Just as we did in those early Costco days when Gerri, my wife, worked the membership desk at our first warehouse in Seattle, we did a lot of talking about exactly what might be possible. We had come to realize something: Unless this was a national campaign and raised an enormous amount of money, nobody was going to pay any attention to it.

So we began talking about how much money it would take (and where we'd get it) to make a real difference to thousands of students—and how we could help these students earn their degrees. We set the goal at a billion dollars to help kids get scholarships. At $30,000 per student in 2006 dollars over 4 or 5 years, we'd be able to help 40,000 students earn their undergraduate degrees over the course of two decades.

We'd mention a billion dollars and people would look at us and roll their eyes. They probably thought we were crazy. Maybe in a

5

Raising a Billion Dollars

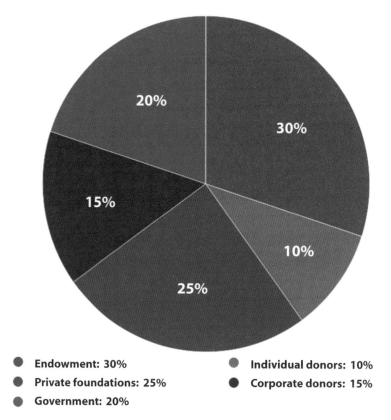

- ● Endowment: 30%
- ● Private foundations: 25%
- ● Government: 20%
- ● Individual donors: 10%
- ● Corporate donors: 15%

way we were. Sure, it wouldn't be easy. I knew rejection would become commonplace. But impossible? No way—especially not when the problems were so serious, tuitions were soaring and the needs were so overwhelming.

Before the third meeting I met with Jim Sinegal, the CEO and President of Costco. Jim has always been sensitive to broader social needs. He and I talked about how we might be able to help these kids earn their baccalaureate degrees. It is a well-known fact that we can educate ourselves out of poverty. But to raise money for this education, first this truth has to be understood and embraced by those people who have more than most.

We both lamented the fact that in the state of Washington we had many high-paying jobs that required a baccalaureate degree or higher, and that most of these jobs were being filled by individuals from out of state or even from out of the country.

As one of Washington's leading employers, hiring across a full spectrum of positions, Jim was particularly attuned to the challenge of hiring workers for a wide variety of positions and across various educational levels. We both agreed something needed to be done.

Given my career at Costco, it was incredibly difficult to talk about going in a different direction after being focused on the company for 17 years. Jim was not only understanding, but completely supportive. What's more, he said that he and Jeff Brotman, the Chairman of Costco, wanted to do an annual breakfast fundraiser to help students of color go either to Seattle University or to the University of Washington.

This was a great idea. Through previous work with the Zion Academy breakfast, we had experience with the concept which supported activities in their preschool-to-8th grade programs. Plus, because of Initiative 200, which reversed affirmative action in Washington state, schools could no longer actively recruit minority students as they might have done in the past. However, they *could* accept private contributions from organizations that were donated for this purpose.

> Over the six years Costco has sponsored its annual breakfast, more than $10 million has been raised to help minority students attend the University of Washington and Seattle University.

So we began to strategize about how this fundraising initiative would work, and soon launched our first benefit breakfast in September 2000—raising $1.2 million. It was more than we imagined, more than we had even hoped for in our dreams. Clearly, thinking big had paid off! And our success with the Costco breakfast continues to this day. In 2005—Costco's sixth annual breakfast—thanks to all the executives at Costco, the amount raised was over $2.4 million.

Jim and Jeff were great supporters from the start, but by now there were just a handful of us left who were focused on that 15th recommendation of the Commission, including former Governor and Senator Dan Evans, Bill Gates Sr., Sam Smith (then the President of Washington State University), Lee Huntsman (who was representing Dick McCormick, the former President of the University of Washington), and Ann Ramsay-Jenkins, who was serving with me on the Higher Education Coordinating Board for the state of Washington and who later became my partner and co-founder at the Foundation. Ann was actually working on a similar track, and had been exploring the idea of setting up a quasi-public/ private foundation with operational management, working like the Port Authority of New York.

We were down to a core group of highly enthusiastic individuals, the ones who weren't too busy to commit their time and energy to this process.

The night after our third meeting, Bill Gates Sr. gave me a call. "The Gates Foundation might have some interest in getting involved," he informed me. "Why don't you give Dr. Deborah Wilds a call tomorrow—she's the person who's behind our scholarship initiatives."

At 8:01 the next morning, I called Dr. Wilds. (To be honest, I didn't sleep much the night before!)

It was clear from the start that while the Gates Foundation had the potential to be incredibly generous; they were also going to demand the highest performance in terms of both objectives and results. As a Costco guy, the Gates Foundation's high standards were those I could understand and respect.

The first thing we had to do was to frame the problem precisely. With the help of people like Becki Collins and Linda Lamar of the Higher Education Coordinating Board, we had access to a lot of useful data on education.

We knew, for example, that 60,000 kids graduated from high

school in the state of Washington in 1999. A lot of those children—more than 20,000—had dropped out of high school before graduating. A tragedy. In our view, we'd already lost

> Washington's high school graduation rate of 68.5% places it 36th among all states.

far too many kids who had dropped out of high school, most of them never to return.

Of the 60,000 kids who did graduate, only about half of them continued their education upon graduation. That's 28,000 who did *not* go to college. We asked ourselves: how many of those 28,000 kids could be successful if they simply had the money to continue their education? The place where we felt our organization could have the most impact was with the students who did indeed make it through four years of high school and truly possessed a desire to succeed.

We knew there were plenty of reasons why some of those kids weren't college candidates. Some of them had scraped by in high school and were lucky to get their diplomas. Some of them had plenty of family resources, but not an educational temperament.

But a lot of them—somewhere between 6,000 and 12,000 students every year—weren't going to college or were dropping out of college simply because they didn't have the money to pay for it.

Lack of money. It was the only thing standing in the way of these young men and women getting a college education. They had the brains; they had the desire. But given the costs of education and other challenges, they didn't have the hope.

We knew these 6,000 to 12,000 young people could succeed if they just had the chance. All of them had financial challenges. But very few of them had family members who had gone to college. That was where the problems began, since these kids didn't have role models in the form of adults who could advise them on all the complicated things that a young person considering college has to work through—from dealing with the application process to selecting the right school. I think it's hard for those of us who have been raised in middle-class environments to truly appreciate all the challenges that some of these lower-income children face.

Many of them do quite well in school—but they're not all straight-A students or stellar athletes. Some of them deal with tremendous challenges every day in their home lives that seem almost unbelievable in our modern society—from neglect to family violence. Many of them come from wonderfully loving families, but without education there's not much hope that either Mom or Dad can get anything much beyond a minimum-wage job. They might each work two jobs just to pay for basic necessities. It certainly doesn't provide them with enough to pay for college.

As a result, we knew we needed to do more than just throw money at the problem. We needed to put a host of resources into the effort, starting with kids during the high school years, *before* they lost the hope of going to college and were lost.

As we framed the problem in the spring of 2000, the Gates Foundation had encouraged us to "think big," so we put together a far-reaching proposal that would be available to students across the state.

In early July of 2000, our proposal was rejected. Still, we were not discouraged. And in fact, Bill Gates Sr. invited us to go back and rework our initial ideas around some programs that their foundation had already under way to redesign a select number of high schools in particularly needy areas. We went back to the drawing board.

On Halloween—which happens to be Ann Ramsay-Jenkins' birthday—we got an invitation to a meeting at the Gates Foundation. Greeting Ann with a special cake and an album for collecting mementos, Bill Gates Sr. informed us that the Washington Education Foundation would receive a hundred-million-dollar grant for a ten-year scholarship program.

Suddenly, the dream of helping those 6,000 to 12,000 kids every year had become a reality. And all at once, both Ann and I knew we had committed ourselves for the next ten years.

Scholarship Programs

Working with our partners in leading corporations and in the benefactor community, the Washington Education Foundation has created five scholarship funds which have already made it possible for more than 3,000 deserving students to attend college.

Each scholarship fund is unique, with its own set of opportunities and requirements. Our goal is to maintain the flexibility that will allow us to best meet the needs both of the benefactor organizations and the scholarship recipients.

Because of the established working relationships between our outstanding staff and many of the leading educators, benefactors, and volunteers throughout the state, we're able to efficiently distribute funds in a way that most effectively supports students and contributes to their success throughout their college experience.

Under some scholarship programs, the organizations we work with depend on us to select high-potential recipients and to manage all the details of each student scholarship.

In other cases, such as the Leadership 1000 Scholarship fund, the individual or organization may choose to become closely involved not only by establishing the guidelines for the actual scholarship, but also by maintaining ongoing contact with the student as well.

Each fund is different, but we're extremely pleased with the results of them all. They give these wonderful students something that they wouldn't have otherwise: hope. And the promise of a better life.

So far, we've been pleased with the success rates of our programs. But we think we can do even better.

For example, since we initiated the Achievers Scholarship program in 2001, we've had about 500 new students attend college each year. We've been happy to see that the Achievers Scholars are staying in college at much higher rates than they would have had they tried to do it on their own without the resources provided by the Bill & Melinda Gates Foundation and the assistance provided by the Washington Education Foundation.

We now expect about 60 percent of our first group of Achievers Scholars, most of whom began college in the fall of 2001, to receive their four-year college degrees. This compares to a typical four-year college graduation rate of about 25 percent for low-income students. Although this graduation rate is impressive, it is not good enough. The goal of the Washington Education Foundation and the Bill & Melinda Gates Foundation is to see that at least 75 percent of the Achievers Scholars receive their four-year degrees.

Because of what we've learned and how our programs have evolved, we believe that each successive group of Achievers Scholars will graduate at a higher rate than the previous group. The enrollees in the second class, for example, continued on at a rate that was 3 percent higher as of the fall term of their junior year. Although this is a modest increase, the cumulative effects of increases like this each year will have a huge impact in the numbers of students who graduate in the years to come.

Admittedly it's almost impossible to imagine, but we would not be surprised to see our tenth and final group of Achievers Scholars with a college graduation rate of 80 to 90 percent!

ACHIEVERS SCHOLARSHIP

Working closely with the Bill & Melinda Gates Foundation, over the past five years and for the next five years, we have and will provide more than $100 million for scholarships to 5,000 Washington state students. The preparation for these scholarships— which are available to students from 16 selected high schools with high percentages of low-income students—begins with high school juniors, through programs designed to assist students through the college selection and application process. In addition to financial support, the students are provided with college mentors who guide scholarship recipients from high school to college.

The Achievers Scholarship program is a comprehensive program that provides four to five years of significant scholarship funding to each student and also provides a six-year support network of high school academic, mentoring and personal support, constant Foundation staff assistance, and two years of college mentoring support.

Thanks to the incredible generosity of the Gates Foundation, we were able to fast-start this program, giving the first scholarships within months of receiving the grant. Achievers Scholarships are typically given to students during their junior year, so that they have their full senior year to prepare for college. In that first year, however, we gave out scholarships to both juniors and seniors simply because we felt that it was more equitable to our initial crop of students. It also meant we had to work doubly hard to get those students on track.

As the program has evolved, there are many factors which have contributed to ever-increasing retention and graduation rates among Achievers Scholars, including:

- A multi-stage scholarship selection process that incorporates many different factors—including several non-cognitive evaluations that aren't strictly tied to each student's grade-point average, which may have been affected by a variety of factors such as family environments and challenges that made it difficult for students to focus on grades while they attended high school.

- Assistance from their high school "Hometown Mentors" and College Preparatory Advisors—a critical part of the program which, as we'll discuss later, has eased the transition into college for these students, many of whom are the first generation of young people in their families to attend college.

- Participation by all scholarship recipients in the Achievers College Experience (ACE) summer program— a program in which new scholarship recipients, having completed their junior year in high school, spend a week during summer at a college campus learning about the entire college application process and the college opportunities available to them in the state of Washington.

- Higher expectations from teachers and parents so that they don't stagnate in an educational limbo, uncertain what the future may hold or what the specific value of their high school education might be.

- More emphasis on taking college-prep courses in the high schools—classes which many of these students might otherwise have been discouraged from taking.

- Scholarship assistance that averages $25,000 per student over four or five years

- Helping to meet students' full financial needs after other federal, state and private financial aid programs are first considered. Like other scholarship programs overseen by the Washington Education Foundation, our emphasis is on the "last-dollar in"—in other words, we bridge the gap in available scholarship money and ultimately tip the scale so that the student has the full amount of resources necessary for a college education.

- Eliminating or reducing the need for Achievers Scholars to take out student loans which, as we'll discuss later, are viewed suspiciously by students from families of many cultures; and are potentially a serious burden to the student if he or she does not manage to complete a college education.

- Our committed Foundation staff members, along with the Gates Foundation, work closely with the students, both before they enter college, and in their transition into and through the college experience.
- The ongoing support of College Mentors who provide additional support to the students as they enter and attend college, ensuring that their education gets on the right track right away and stays on track until graduation.
- Finally—and this can't be overlooked—the enthusiastic participation of older Achievers Scholars who have stepped forward to serve as role models and motivate the younger Achievers Scholars who are just entering the program.

This is also part of a larger Gates Foundation effort in which they push to have every high school graduate college-ready. With all these terrific program resources and support services we expect to triple each student's chances of earning a college degree.

Once they complete their education, these students—now equipped with their four-year college degrees—will be in a position to give back much to their communities, to the state of Washington and to future generations of high school students like themselves.

While none of this would have been possible without the time, commitment and resources provided by the Gates Foundation, we also recognize that to grow and succeed this program must ultimately receive the support of other organizations as well—similar to the support the Gates Foundation has given for other programs, such as the Higher Education Readiness Opportunity (HERO) initiative that supports college education for underrepresented populations. In one sense, we think of the Gates Foundation grant as seed money that allowed us to start up these programs. Now, as we look forward, we're working with state and local community

Painted Sky Warrior
Achievers Scholar

THE FIRST QUESTION EVERYONE ALWAYS ASKS IS, "WHAT'S WITH THE NAME?"

His dad was Native American, his mom Scotch/Irish. For a month after he was born, they just called him "boy."

Then one evening, a rainbow reached across the sky and a cloud shaped like a turtle wafted by in the sunset. Behind the turtle chased another cloud, shaped like a warrior, which appeared to be waving at them.

Painted Sky Warrior had his name. A name of unquestioned nobility, but it didn't make his life any easier as his family moved from one small town to another, looking for a way of making ends meet and a place to call home. As a child, he never knew if next month he'd be in California or Oregon or Washington or Idaho or British Columbia, nor did it matter.

Sky always had to explain about the name, and with a name like that, he could never conceal his Native American heritage, especially when he faced discrimination.

His parents separated when he was in seventh grade and he settled with his dad—a disabled Vietnam veteran—in north central Washington. It was the first time he'd ever lived in one place for more than a year.

The money didn't come easy. His dad, being 100 percent disabled, couldn't maintain steady employment; the veteran's checks only brought in a few hundred dollars a month. So even as a teenager, Sky had to work to keep his family afloat.

He got to be good at construction work but he never had time to be especially good at school. It's not that he wasn't smart, he was just busy. He took a lot of teasing from friends who never completely understood why he didn't have as much time as they did to party.

A fourth-grade teacher had inspired Sky with an appreciation of Japanese culture. It was a driving force in his life—he learned some of the language, practiced Aikido, and studied a lot about the country and the people. Some day, some way, he told himself, he'd make it to Japan to see it for himself.

Sky always dreamed he'd go to college. Once he even told his parents he would some day attend his favorite school, Notre Dame, but knew he could never afford to do it. One day the principal at his high school made an announcement that a new Achievers Scholarship was available that would help to pay for a college education. "All of you should apply for it," he told the students.

So Sky signed up, figuring he really didn't have much of a chance. For once, Sky was wrong. Given the opportunity, he was able to demonstrate not only his exceptional personality, but his innate intelligence as well. He earned an Achievers Scholarship, and is now attending Washington State University with a double major in International Business and Business Management and minoring in both Japanese and Finance.

Next year he'll be campaigning for student body president of Washington State University—an endeavor he never would have imagined pursuing; an opportunity provided to him by the Achievers Scholarship.

If not for his Achievers Scholarship, Sky might have continued in the carpentry trade, his potential never realized. With this scholarship, he's in a position to help change the world.

Inspired by Sky's success, his sister was also accepted by Washington State University. Sky's hoping his other siblings will follow in her path. "Our parents are so proud and supportive," he says. "Watching our success makes them truly happy."

leaders to establish an ongoing fund that will allow us to continue building on this infrastructure for decades to come.

COSTCO SCHOLARSHIP

As a key element in its commitment to excellence in higher education, Costco has raised more than $10 million through its annual breakfast event to make it possible for students of color to attend Seattle University or the University of Washington.

Each year, Costco puts together an annual fundraising breakfast attended by nearly 1,000 participants, which features noteworthy speakers such as last year's Lieutenant Colonel (Retired) Consuelo Kickbusch and the year before "The Three Doctors"—three black medical professionals, two MDs and one dentist—who are giving back their time and energy to their communities after escaping an impoverished upbringing. You'll read more about The Three Doctors later in this book—it's an amazing story.

What's more, several students serve as speakers at these breakfasts. Their personal stories—always amazing, often touching—help to provide a perspective on the value of the Costco Scholarship and its meaning to them personally as well as to the community at large. Additional Costco Scholarship students are sitting at each table and sharing their stories one-on-one with attendees.

The attendees at this annual Costco event include leading figures in the Washington state community, political leaders, Costco vendors and friends, and a variety of other people from the Seattle community who are concerned about educational issues and the impact education has in shaping the future of our society and the business community.

Costco has asked the Washington Education Foundation to manage some of the details involved with organizing the event itself, as well as to facilitate the coordination of funds with the recipient universities. It works out well for both of us—Costco can look to us to help keep the details of their outstanding event going smoothly; we can assist Costco in its laudable efforts to ensure that these campuses will reflect the diversity of our broader community.

In fact, that's something we've heard time and again from the universities themselves: The event has not only opened up opportunities for the scholarship recipients but has also brought broader benefits to their campuses by increasing diversity.

CHÂTEAU STE. MICHELLE SCHOLARSHIP

To support diversity at the University of Washington and Washington State University, Château Ste. Michelle sponsors a special annual dinner concert each year at its beautiful grounds in Woodinville, Washington. Proceeds from the event provide diversity scholarships for students at both universities.

What's particularly notable about this program is that it combines the best of both worlds—a great concert featuring well-known musicians for people to enjoy, along with the opportunity for the people who attend the concert to know that they're supporting a good cause.

Another positive feature of this concert event is that it brings in a lot of people who, frankly, may otherwise not have participated in an educationally focused fundraiser. They come for the good music, but they leave with the knowledge that they've also been able to have a part in doing some good.

GOVERNOR'S SCHOLARSHIP

Recognizing that children in foster, group, and kinship care face special challenges when they reach age 18—in particular, the lack of any family or public funding—in 2001 Governor Gary Locke initiated the Governor's Scholarship Program to make it possible for these children to attend college.

The program has been a resounding success. An annual Governor's Cup Charity Golf Tournament has raised nearly a million and a half dollars over the past few years to support students "aging out" of foster care. Governor Locke is now joined by our new Governor, Christine Gregoire, to continue this very important event.

Additionally, the event has raised awareness of the special challenges and needs faced by foster children who are often left adrift when they leave foster care. Many have already faced difficult challenges—often due to family violence, drugs, or sexual assault. All too often in the foster-care system, children may be transferred from home to home and school to school, frequently for reasons unrelated to their personal situation. Occasionally they may be re-united with their original families, only to be separated again.

All of this makes it particularly difficult for children raised in foster care to earn stellar grades in school. Later, when thrust into the world at age 18, college appears to be an impossible goal.

Nothing could be farther from the truth. In fact, we've already seen that the large majority of former foster children who receive a Governor's Scholarship are quite capable of success. In a sense, they've already been through the tough "school of hard knocks" in their lives. Many have become extraordinarily capable of the kind of flexibility and focus they'll need for college. Thanks to the Governor's Scholarship Program, more and more of Washington's foster youth are getting the chance to show what they can accomplish in a college setting.

LEADERSHIP 1000 SCHOLARSHIP

Our newest scholarship program is designed so that individuals, businesses, families, corporations and other organizations can support low-income students by providing personalized scholarships. This is a real one-to-one program in which benefactors are able to shape their tax-deductible contributions any way they want, directing the Foundation to identify students from a particular high school, college, or major area of study.

Our goal with the Leadership 1000 program is to ultimately

support a thousand students, moving from a few initial recipients to approximately 250 each year.

A law firm, for example, might fund a scholarship at the university where the principals of the firm studied or at a school in the firm's local community. A person wanting to create a memorial scholarship might direct that it be offered at the high school attended by the departed person. One benefactor figured supporting a student was the perfect birthday gift for his wife—a civic-minded individual who was committed to education.

A company interested in contributing to the progress of science might direct that their scholarship be offered to a student studying physics, or an individual interested in promoting the performing arts might direct that their scholarship be offered to a student in music, acting, or dance. The benefactors set the parameters; the Foundation makes the selection of the actual student recipients.

Because each donation is linked directly to a particular student, benefactors have the opportunity to meet their students and follow students' individual progress through college if they choose. To recognize contributions, scholarships can be established in a family or company name or, if preferred, remain anonymous.

The value of the Leadership 1000 Scholarship is two-fold:

1. It allows benefactors to see the direct benefit of their donations and how a specific contribution helps an individual student, rather than placing donations into a general scholarship fund.

2. In some cases, it also allows the Foundation to support students that may have special circumstances that would not fall directly into one of our other scholarship programs. For example, we might be able to support an undocumented student or a student who has extraordinary financial needs that would prevent him or her from continuing in college.

Admittedly, this scholarship requires a financial commitment from the benefactor—anywhere from $5,000 to $10,000 a year over the four to five years it takes for a student to complete a college education. As a foundation, we realize we have to select benefactors for this program with the same care we use to select students. It is important that the benefactor be prepared to make the full commitment, because we do not want to create a situation in which a student loses a scholarship halfway through college.

We like to think of the Leadership 1000 Scholarship Program as a great investment in the future, and a program that can change the life of many a student today.

2

UNDERSTANDING NEEDS, FACING HARSH REALITIES

ON JUNE 22ND, 1944, PRESIDENT FRANKLIN D. ROOSEVELT signed the Serviceman's Readjustment Act of 1944, better known as the GI Bill.

It was a landmark piece of legislation. Not only did it provide billions of dollars in low-interest education and home loans to returning veterans of World War II, but it was color blind as well, granting rights equally to all returning soldiers who had served at least three months during the war.

We usually talk about this bill as a way the nation paid tribute and gave thanks to those who had risked their lives overseas. But there was another purpose to it as well. Before the war, the country had suffered the worst economic depression in its history. As the war wound to a close, many people feared that the return of 16 million soldiers into the workplace would mean the return of soup lines, massive unemployment, and widespread poverty.

The GI Bill was originally conceived to prevent the possibility of an economic collapse when the soldiers came home. Servicemen and women would be offered the opportunity to attend college, which not only reduced the potential shock of suddenly adding millions of new people into the workforce, but also opened the possibility that future workforces would be more highly skilled and trained than in the past.

The bill succeeded beyond almost anyone's expectations. More than 2 million former soldiers were able to attend college, while 6 million others took advantage of other educational and training opportunities. Before the bill was passed, there had been concerns that flooding the universities might result in lower educational standards. But the exact opposite happened. While some schools may have had to put up temporary buildings and Quonset huts to deal with the influx of new students, they discovered that the addition of these older students of all cultures and socioeconomic backgrounds actually improved the diversity and maturity of their campuses, and led to better and more well-rounded educational experiences for everyone.

What's more, in the process of providing these young men and women with better educational opportunities, the GI Bill also provided them with better opportunities after they graduated.

Better education meant better jobs. Better jobs meant that more of them could afford homes. Broader home ownership helped to foster the growth of the middle class. And that virtuous cycle continued, helping to spark the greatest era of economic growth in our country's history.

The result of that economic growth has benefited all of us today. It may have started with a GI Bill that was designed around the specific needs of veterans, but the implications of that legislation has been much more far-reaching. The GI Bill is a perfect example of how supporting education can have positive benefits that go well beyond just the people who are actually educated. By establishing a pro-active program to educate those soldiers who came out of World War II, we not only benefited them, but our entire society as well.

Before that era, only the wealthy could afford to go to college. Changing that equation and opening up the universities to more students ultimately meant that our country was able to accomplish amazing things that just a few years before would have been considered impossible.

In many ways, the GI Bill was the model for what we did when we instituted the Washington Education Foundation in Washington state. We knew that each year thousands of low-income students in Washington graduated from high school but did not enroll in college. Thousands more enrolled in college but did not complete a bachelor's degree.

With a relatively small level of support—partly financial, partly in guidance and mentoring—most of these students

> The GI Bill is a perfect example of how supporting education can have positive benefits that go well beyond just the people who are actually educated.

could succeed, and ultimately be equipped to contribute their skills, their talents, and their energies to society. As with the GI Bill, we'd all benefit.

But under the current system, we all lose out when these students don't make it to college or don't make it through a four-year program.

When broken down into demographic groups, there are some notable ways to determine which students are most likely to obtain bachelor's degrees:

- Women are more likely to succeed than men.
- Asian and White students are more likely to succeed than Hispanics, Blacks or Native Americans.
- Children of parents with some post-secondary education and/or children living in two-parent households are more likely to get a degree than those from families in which the parents did not attend college or households in which there is only one parent.

In addition, there are several definable groups that face extraordinary struggles that too often preclude them from attending college. Foster children, for example, are supported by the state until the age of 18 and then they are on their own, without any source of income or any family support structure.

It's said they're "emancipated out of foster care," but it's hardly a feeling of freedom. In fact, many of these kids go through the same sense of loss that they experienced when they lost or were taken from their original families.

Most of us, raised in more traditional households, never had to face such challenges and never had to be completely out on our own at such a young age. Even if we had to work our way through college, we always had a home and a support structure to fall back on. But these kids have to make their own way in the world, completely alone, and at a very tender age.

As noted earlier, there are many children who have been raised in impoverished households who simply never get the nutrition they need from day to day; they are dependent on the school lunch program and other public programs. They're a world apart from the idyllic fantasies of *Father Knows Best*, Beaver Cleaver, and *Happy Days*. For these children, the world can be a very tough place.

All too many kids, lacking the financial resources to attend college, are pushed by well-meaning counselors to join the military as a way to earn a college scholarship when they're discharged. I applaud those young men and women who choose a career of military service to our country and are willing to put their lives on the line in our defense. At the same time, it doesn't seem fair and it isn't smart public policy to push people into military service just because it's the only way they can pay for college. Plus, we lose too many of these young people when they leave the military. Although most may have entered the service with the good intention of continuing their education, after their tour of duty many choose instead to go to work and get on with the responsibilities of their lives.

All of these are, quite simply, the children left behind. It's said that for every action there's an equal and opposite reaction. But in the world of education, it's *inaction* that leads to problems. Many scholarship programs pride themselves on supporting the best and the brightest. Undeniably, these are students that deserve and often need our support. But to have a real impact on society, we need to think about the other 95 percent of students—the ones that may have less-than-perfect grades and only better-than-decent SAT scores.

Grades and tests are only two measures of an individual student's potential abilities. (They're still important, mind you, and I'd encourage any student reading this book to attempt to do his or her best on them!) Still, there are many factors that can lead to students facing grade problems. If their home environment isn't stable, it's hard to imagine that their grades will be stellar. And if a student's family is struggling to make ends meet or to put food on the table or if parents have to work night shifts, it's hard for them to pay much attention to helping their children with homework. What's more, English isn't the primary language spoken in many of the homes of the students we support, so many parents couldn't understand the homework even if they did have time for it. Parents who believe that education is the key to a better life for their children often never found that key themselves and don't really know the best way to guide their children.

There are many other factors that can have an impact on a student's grades as well. Peer pressure, for example, often has too much influence on an impressionable young person. If it isn't considered "cool" to get good grades, too many children will opt out of learning all too early in their lives. We'd all like it more if these students rose above peer pressure and applied themselves earlier, but it is a reality that some of these young people are too influenced by their environment.

If our society doesn't do something to break this cycle, we'll

Olatokunbo Olaniya
Achievers Scholar

GROWING UP FAST

Even as a young woman, Olatokunbo faced challenges that would floor most of us. She had a mom so sick she couldn't care for her children. Her stepdad was abusive, and left the picture when her mother became ill. Huge financial challenges forced the family to balance the need for medicine with rent and food.

As a teenager, when many girls her age were thinking mostly about make-up and prom dates, Olatokunbo had to be responsible, caring for her mother and her younger sister.

Her mother's illness was, she notes, the greatest hardship she'd ever had to endure. For two years, her mother was on the brink of death. Olatokunbo took on the responsibility of serving as her nurse, as well as being her mom's arms and legs to do those things that her mother couldn't do herself.

She wanted to go to college. She already knew what she wanted to do as an adult. At age 11 she had met a woman who worked as a prosecuting attorney, who inspired her with the realization of how she could make a difference in the world, by becoming part of the solution instead of crumbling under all the problems.

But she didn't know how she'd ever get to college. Not only was money an issue, but there was no college tradition in her background, so she really didn't know the steps required for getting into and paying for a four-year school.

In her junior year of high school, she heard about the Achievers Scholarship program. A counselor explained how the program worked, and connected her with a mentor who helped shepherd her application through the process. Olatokunbo decided to attend Gonzaga University.

So far, so good. But like many young people from disadvantaged backgrounds, the first year of college wasn't easy for her. Not only did she have to deal with the culture shock of suddenly being in a big school far away from home and facing a high standard of academic requirements, but she carried with her the additional burden of wanting to do everything she could to make life easier for her mom and sister.

She almost didn't make it. Unbeknownst to many of us, Olatokunbo took on a couple of jobs and was working 40-plus hours a week—in part, because she's always been a very driven young woman, but also so that she could help her mom.

It was a balancing act that went way beyond the call of duty. Pamila Gant, the College Relations Officer at the Washington Education Foundation, heard of Olatokunbo's situation and intervened. This wouldn't have been possible without the presence of a College Mentor—an on-campus adviser who could monitor what was happening.

The first two years in college can be particularly hard on any student; it is the time when the pressures of education and life make it more likely a student will drop out. Without someone providing, not only money, but guidance and support to young people like Olatokunbo, we'd lose a lot more students.

Pamila Gant brought me into the picture and, even more importantly, introduced my wife Gerri to Olatokunbo. Gerri is a Gonzaga trustee and was able to make a personal commitment to helping Olatokunbo succeed.

I am happy to report that she made it. In fact, she succeeded beyond our highest expectations. She was accepted to eight law schools across the country, ultimately deciding to attend Syracuse University where she'll continue on the path to her lifelong dream.

still be dealing with these problems for generations to come.

Experts have long argued that there are cultural biases in grading and SAT scores as well—and whether that's true or not, it's clear we have some tough cultural realities to face.

Individuals who grow up without education are much more likely to get stuck in low-paying dead-end jobs. The work isn't fulfilling; their futures aren't secure. Some percentage of these people will opt out of working at all and choose lives of crime and violence instead.

I would encourage everyone to read the books by the Three Doctors, who are profiled later in Chapter 5. As young people, they grew up in a New Jersey ghetto. The symbols of success in their community were the drug dealers—who dressed well and always seemed to have enough money to spend—and the gang members— who commanded fear and respect from everyone around them. They were hardly good role models, but they're the only role models that many urban children like them see growing up.

Worse, though, is the fact that we seem to be caught in a never-ending cycle: raising kids in poverty who learn the hard lessons of the streets far too early in their lives, who make too many mistakes too early. Many of them end up in prison, and the children they give birth to are no better off than their parents, facing sometimes even more violence and more difficult challenges.

We can break this cycle, as long as we recognize it for what it is, and commit ourselves to getting past it. Education alone won't break the cycle—there are no easy solutions, and the problems are far too complex—but without the hope of education, there really isn't any hope that people can escape poverty, violence, and lives of great hardship.

Each year in the state of Washington approximately 6,000 low-income high school graduates, who could succeed if they had the chance, do not enroll in a post-secondary program. Low-income students face a number of barriers that preclude them from attending college after their high school graduation or from successfully graduating from college with a bachelor's degree. These factors include the stark fact that **college is not affordable**: For low-income families, the cost of sending their children to a four-year public institution can appear daunting. The average annual cost for attending college can be 62 percent of a typical poor family's annual income. And as indicated on the website of *The Princeton Review*, annual average costs for tuition, room and board plus fees are going to become even more expensive over the next two decades, growing at approximately 5 percent per year. At the same time the cost of attending college is going up, the financial support for students has been decreasing. Look, for example, at how state support for higher education has eroded in the state of Washington:

State Spending per Budgeted FTE Student Will Increase in the 2007 - 2009 Biennium

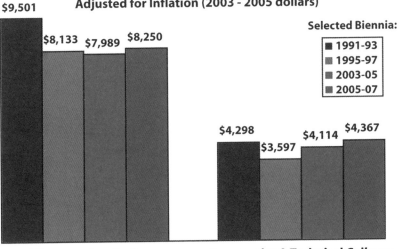

State Appropriations per Budgeted FTE Student
Adjusted for Inflation (2003 - 2005 dollars)

$9,501
$8,133 $7,989 $8,250

Selected Biennia:
■ 1991-93
■ 1995-97
■ 2003-05
■ 2005-07

$4,298
$3,597
$4,114 $4,367

Public 4-year Institutions   **Community & Technical Colleges**

(Washington State figures)

While scholarship programs are working hard to keep up with increasing costs and decreasing support, low-income families are often unaware of financial aid programs and the availability of scholarships, and therefore perceive college as unaffordable. The result is that their sons and daughters don't even try. This defeatist attitude goes all the way back to which classes those students select to take in high school in the first place.

Even when financial aid is available, the additional costs associated with attending college—paying for basic necessities like food and clothing—can be prohibitive for low-income students and families with no savings or discretionary income to draw upon.

There is a lack of academic preparation. What's worse is the fact that it's a never-ending cycle. High school students who want to attend a four-year college need to prepare themselves academically by taking college preparatory courses. But because of financial limitations, many students and their families dismiss the option of going to college relatively early in their K–12 experience and never see the value of taking a college preparatory curriculum. Plus, many low-income students face academic challenges even from the point at which they first enter high school—years before they have to make college-bound decisions. For example, only 18 percent of Washington's low-income eighth-graders were proficient in reading in 2003, compared to 33 percent of students of all incomes. These students require remedial course work and support to become college-ready. High schools provide limited support and encouragement to make up the lost ground which often results from a combination of low expectations, lack of a drive to succeed from the students themselves and their families, and limited resources available to schools for funding remedial academics or college preparatory courses.

Most high school students are given insufficient information about college. In Washington state the courses required to graduate from high school are different from those required for entry into a four-year college. Therefore, it is critical that students are given adequate information early on in their high school years about the course requirements for college attendance. Students also need to be informed about what is required for the college application process and how to navigate their way through financial-aid programs.

Many low-income students rely on their schools to give them this kind of information and often these schools have an inadequate college advising system to provide this service. In some schools, counselors may have to support hundreds of students, making it almost impossible for them to focus on the needs of any individual student. Remedial work and gathering information on college requirements can represent a special burden for those students who require more time to get college-ready. Such lack of information and the needed remedial work can mean that students are not prepared for college nor do they decide to apply to college.

There can be a lack of motivation. All high school students require a high degree of motivation and encouragement to enroll in and attend a four-year college. The impetus for this motivation often comes from adult role models who can speak to all the benefits of the college experience. For many low-income students, these role models do not exist in their homes or in their local communities. Such students may even find themselves in an environment that may discourage any college ambitions, either due to family pressures to go to work or peer pressure and social biases against high academic standards.

Teachers can be a source of encouragement for low-income students, but they often focus their limited time on those students who are already motivated towards college when they enter high school. As a result, many low-income students do not prepare academically or financially for a four-year college and thus they lose the opportunity to attend.

To compound the problem, those students who *do* manage to attend some college but *do not complete* a bachelor's degree face additional challenges.

Of course, there are the financial challenges. For many low-income families, sending their children to college creates a financial burden that cannot be sustained. Even with the financial aid that is available, families struggle to pay for books, transportation and food. In addition, some students continue to work to contribute to the family income even while attending classes. These situations often force low-income students to raise funds through loans or other means. For many, the financial pressure will lead them to drop out when they can no longer increase their debt burden. Sometimes other urgent family financial issues require them to work full-time. Often, they have to work so many hours every week that they cannot sustain their academic performance and, as a result, they lose their federal and state need grants.

For many children who live in low-income homes, post-secondary education is simply not considered a possibility. While some scholarships exist, many worthy students don't know the procedures to access them. What's more, most of the available scholarships cover only a portion of the cost of attending college, requiring the students to apply for loans as well if there is no other financial source.

A typical student attending a university would need to borrow between $5,000 to $7,000 each year, even with scholarships. But many low-income families would not consider permitting their children to borrow at these levels, particularly for the five years it takes a typical student to earn a baccalaureate degree. To understand why, it's important to remember that consumer debt is, quite simply, a middle-class phenomenon. Dr. Jane Jervis, former president of The Evergreen State College, notes:

> "Middle-income families use consumer loans for mortgages, new cars, credit-card purchases, going out to dinner, taking vacations. For very low-income families attending college is itself a big risk with unknown and

unknowable benefits. For them, debt is not the passport to the good life; it is more often associated with foreclosure, eviction, homelessness, and disgrace."

And, as Becki Collins, formerly with the Higher Education Coordinating Board, recently observed:

> "People from low socio-economic backgrounds have typically had no positive experiences in their lives with credit. What they have experienced are examples in their communities of people who bought a car, and then had it taken away in the middle of the night."

To add to this, consider what happens to low-income students who borrow to finance their studies and then, for any of several reasons, don't finish their programs. The benefit of a college education really doesn't pay off for most people until after they graduate. Frankly, the kids who borrow money to pay for their education can end up with no degree and a potentially huge debt to repay. Is it any surprise that their families discourage them from taking out loans?

College-bound students need orientation and support. All high school students who attend a four-year college face huge transitions in their lives. Students are confronted with a move to a new community, a new and larger population of peers, new learning structures, and a need to be more independent. For many low-income students this new environment is overwhelming as they struggle to assimilate. They may be the first generation in their families to go to college and do not know what to expect once they get there. Many have had limited exposure to environments outside of their communities. Coming from a low-income family can also have the effect of isolating students as they struggle to find peers with similar ethnic, cultural, or socio-economic backgrounds. In these situations, low-income students may lack the confidence to reach out for support. The absence of appropriate orientation and outreach programs for these students creates barriers to success.

College-bound students require academic preparation. Many low-income students come from high schools that do not provide the academic rigor or the skills they need to be successful in a college environment. College-bound students need to be able to manage their own schedules and undertake the independent study required for the courses in which they enroll. Low-income students may become overwhelmed by these requirements as they struggle to catch up academically with their peers. As a result, many students end up facing academic failure for the first time, which damages their self-confidence and their resolve to persist. Even if it's just in a class or two, failure can reflect on their self-image and their will to succeed.

College-bound students thrive on family and personal support. Many low-income students face family and/or personal challenges while attending college. These students may require support from social workers and other counselors. This support may not be readily available on campus. Students may leave college prematurely to deal with personal challenges, which may prevent them from sustaining their academic performance. Often they intend to return to college, but once they're dealing with the many challenges of their home environments, it can be difficult for them to get back on the college path.

Many students need assistance to make the transition from a two-year to a four-year track. Some low-income students start their post-secondary education in a community college with the stated goal of transferring to a four-year college in order to complete a bachelor's degree. There are many reasons why low-income students may take this path. They may not be academically prepared for a four-year college; they may lack the financial resources to pay for a four-year college; they may have a family situation requiring them to remain at home or they may not be ready to leave home and the

36

community they know. For students seeking a bachelor's degree, the steps for switching to a four-year institution are highly uncertain; many of the students do not make the transition successfully. To make a successful transition, students need to have good information about the courses that will qualify as prerequisites for a bachelor's degree, how to prepare for the entry exams, and how to attain financial aid. Students often rely on their community colleges to provide them with information and support, but some colleges lack the resources and incentives to assist these students. College advisors are understandably busy, focused on activities and on students' success at the community college campuses, as opposed to preparing those students to go off to other institutions. As a result, only a small percentage of low-income students who begin with the goal of getting a bachelor's degree actually succeed. Furthermore, the students who do make the transition to a four-year college often take more than four years to earn their degrees, and some of them drop out before completion due to financial or personal reasons.

None of this is getting any easier, either. In addition to the barriers for students, the current trends all seem to be moving in the wrong direction—an increasing student population, ballooning costs for higher education, increasing pressure on state budgets for financial aid, and higher education funding, declining Federal Pell Grant purchasing power and an increasing perception of education as a private rather than a public good. All these factors conspire to further increase barriers to bachelor's degree attainment among low-income students.

The Costs to the Students—The Costs to Us All

The consequences of under-education are hard to fathom. A lot of those consequences are practically invisible to most of us—it's the kids that didn't make it who end up performing menial jobs, never knowing that with a college degree life could have been better.

For example, consider the young man profiled in the previous chapter, Painted Sky Warrior. He wasn't an extraordinary high school student, so for years he failed to realize that he had the brains and the talent to reach a world beyond the one he knew. If it weren't for his scholarship, he would have probably been working in a construction job—important work, to be sure, but not in line with his dreams, and not what he was capable of accomplishing. And frankly, Sky is a top-notch and remarkably self-assured kid, someone who now refuses to perceive himself as spiraling down a cycle of failure.

Employment projections indicate that jobs requiring a bachelor's degree will increase by 25 percent by the year 2008, while those requiring only a high school diploma will grow by just 9 percent. Nearly 70 percent of new jobs will require post-secondary education. Those kids who don't escape like Sky did are on a dead-end track.

Job Requirements for Tomorrow

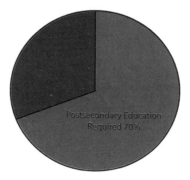

Postsecondary Education
Required 70%

The Educational Testing Service reports that 70% of the new jobs created from 1998 to 2008 nationally will require at least some secondary education.

(Source: Community Research Partners, *Average Isn't Enough: Advancing Working Families to Create an Outstanding Ohio Economy*)

We know that those students who do attend college are more likely to stay out of the unemployment ranks and more likely to earn more money; and, ultimately, college graduates contribute more to the economy and to our society as a whole.

Sometimes when we're feeling altruistic, we talk in terms of educating children out of poverty, breaking the cycle, and leveling the playing field for everybody. These are, we believe, appropriate and noble goals, which people on both sides of the political aisle can embrace (even if approaches for dealing with these challenges may differ). At the same time, however, we believe that there are other societal goals, no less essential and critical, which the

> Recently, 68 percent of Washington employers reported that they had difficulty finding workers with a baccalaureate degree to hire.

educating of a broader base of college students will help us achieve. Most important among these is the one goal that I've mentioned several times already in this book: figuring out how best to educate our workforce for the 21st century, so they can lead the way in defining and creating the future.

This isn't just a task that government needs to take on—instead, it's an essential element for every business of every size to consider. If we are going to be successful in getting the right education and the right training for our workforce, the private sector is going to need to step up to the plate and put its energies—and yes, its financial support—behind this important effort.

If we don't come together as a state and as a nation to better serve our students, we will all suffer the consequences together. We are already seeing the tension created by the high demand and low supply of qualified employees. Recently, 68 percent of Washington employers reported that they had difficulty finding workers with a baccalaureate degree to hire. If employers can't find qualified workers here, they will find them elsewhere. In his recent book *The World is Flat*, Thomas Friedman points out that almost 40 percent of Ph.D.s working in science and engineering positions in the United States are foreign-born.

And yet, on the flip side, the benefits of full participation are profound. One study estimates that increasing minority students' participation in college to the same percentage as their white

Work Experience and Average Annual Earnings of Workers 25 to 64 Years Old by Educational Attainment: 1997 - 1999 (earnings in 1999 dollars)

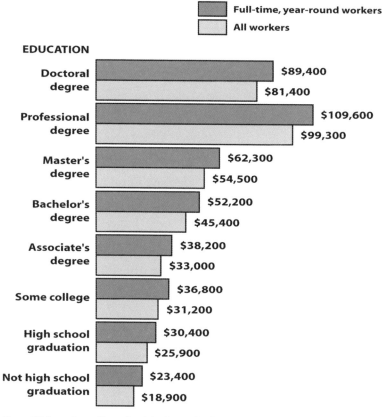

(Source: U.S. Census Bureau, Current Population Surveys, March 1998, 1999, and 2000)

counterparts would create an additional $231 billion in our Gross Domestic Product and at least $80 billion in new tax revenue. That is simply because education and income are closely tied together.

On the other hand, those youths who don't get educated and fall into a downward spiral are the ones who become the more visible victims of the failures brought about under our current system. They may fall prey to other shameful cycles—of drug and alcohol abuse, of crime and sometimes prison. With them, it's not just a case of lost potential, it's a dangerous pattern that not only harms their own lives but damages society at large as well.

And worse, the all-too-typical pattern is that these children end up continuing the cycle of neglect and violence, leading to additional strains on our public resources and adding even more children raised in the same sort of hopeless environment. It is the kind of cycle that ultimately led to the horrible riots, gang violence, and social disruption that make so many people in our society afraid, even in what should be the safety and security of their own homes.

MATH, SCIENCE, AND HEALTHCARE EDUCATION

Recently, there has been a lot of press coverage (along with plenty of fear and criticism) noting our nation's lack of math, science, and healthcare degrees. Quite simply, we don't have enough teachers in these fields nor enough skilled scientists, researchers, mathematicians, and health professionals to meet the needs of the 21st-century workforce.

When we read these reports, it seems like everyone suddenly woke up and discovered a crisis. But the truth is that the crisis has been building for many years. My office is packed with reports from businesses bemoaning the fact that we do not have enough graduates in these fields. Sure, we've pounded on K–12 education in hopes it would turn around the situation. But that hasn't resulted in any improvements. And we haven't come up with any genuinely fresh solutions.

At the Washington Education Foundation we are exploring a very simple strategy of investing in our high school students to increase the number of students majoring in these fields (and, incidentally, also to make the Washington Assessment of Student Learning—the WASL exam—a positive experience).

Visualize a pool of scholarship dollars, raised in both the private and public sectors, earmarked for Washington children who want to major in math and science. If we raised $33 million, we could secure 1,000 scholarships from the Washington state Guaranteed Education Tuition (GET) plan, which would cover complete tuition,

Norma Cueva
Costco Scholar

ALL IN THE FAMILY

Norma has practically become a member of our family. We met her in 2001 when I was making an ad hoc presentation at the Latino/a Educational Achievement Project (LEAP) Conference. LEAP is a program founded in 1998 to help Latina and Latino students in Washington state improve their academic achievement and prepare for college.

Even then, as a senior in high school, Norma knew exactly what she wanted to do in her life. "I want to become a school teacher," she told me, "so I can go back to my hometown and teach kids for whom English is a second language."

I was immediately struck by the confidence and commitment of this wonderful young woman.

Today, four years later, giving back to her community is still her goal. My wife Gerri and I are extremely proud of the fact that we've been able to serve as her mentors and do our little part to help her succeed.

What's more, by keeping to her goal, Norma can do her part to help break the cycle of poverty that so often afflicts migrant families. The children grow up and all too often remain in the fields because of their lack education.

Norma was among the first recipients of the Costco Scholarship. Even though her parents never had the chance to attend college, her dad has always been a big believer in education. He told me that he wanted his kids to enjoy the opportunities he never had.

In that sense, Norma is one of the lucky ones. Many of the students we've supported through the Washington Education Foundation have come from broken homes or homes in which the children had faced terrible circumstances as they grew up. In some cases, low-income parents, unclear about the real value of higher education, put roadblocks in the way of their children. Not Norma's parents—they've truly gone the extra mile to make sure their daughter has every opportunity to reach her dream and to complete her college education.

After meeting Norma, we invited her and her family to visit with us and tour Seattle University. She's always been an excellent student and has kept her focus on her goal since she was 11 years old. Because of her personal drive, Norma might somehow have found her way to attend some college somewhere, but she never imagined she'd have the chance to attend a prestigious private university.

Norma has made the most of her opportunities at Seattle U —not only getting an excellent education, but also taking advantage of the chance to spend part of her junior year in Madrid, Spain.

What's more, she has been actively involved at her school. Among other activities, she has served as president of MEChA, a Latino student organization. She was one of two students selected from her entire senior class to advise and work with the Dean of the College of Arts and Sciences, serving as a representative of the student body. She also helped coordinate the Educated Latinas Leading America Conference at the University.

On Cinco de Mayo last year, her parents came to the Seattle University campus and helped prepare a barbecue for more than 500 people to celebrate the occasion. Given their commitment to Norma and to the opportunities they recognize can evolve from an education, is her success really any surprise?

Norma graduated in 2005 and will begin her master's degree program in teaching this spring.

fees, and additional expenses for these students at any public Washington state university or college. What's more, students with a greater need would also be able to receive additional federal and state grants that are available for low-income students.

We could start by identifying 1,000 10th grade students who perform well on the math and science sections of the WASL. Once we identified these students we would buy each of them a five-year package from the GET plan, which costs about $33,000 today. The GET package would be owned in trust by the Washington Education Foundation so that if the student did not go to college or did not declare math or science as a major, the Foundation could then award this scholarship to another qualified incoming freshman who wanted to follow that path.

By doing this, we could focus these talented students in a direction where their talents are much needed. They could become our future math and science majors. And by making this commitment every year for the foreseeable future, we would begin to graduate a whole new generation of students with high-demand degrees. This would be a *positive* way to use the 10th grade WASL—instead of saddling it with the negative connotations it has today.

Equally important, a strategy like this would help to ensure that the bright 10th-graders would continue to take two more years of advanced science and math and thus be college-ready.

The present total annual cost of this program, before taking into account the annual inflation of the GET cost, would be $33,000,000. That would buy 1,000 math or science majors who would become math and science teachers, scientists and researchers and serve as part of the new workforce of the 21st century.

3

CREATE THE VISION

FROM EARLY ON, OUR VISION STATEMENT has been printed on the back of our business cards:

We provide college scholarships and mentoring to low-income, high-potential students.

We put our mission right there on the card for two reasons. First, it gives us the opportunity to share the Foundation's vision with anyone we meet—from potential benefactors to members of the media, from government officials to college administrators.

The second and more subtle reason our mission is printed on our cards is that it's a reminder for us, too—that we need to be vigilant and focused on this vision each and every day, and that we need to continue to evaluate the choices we make, as well as to review our achievements in terms of how well we accomplish that mission.

I'd learned this at Costco, where our corporate mission was always clear and focused:

To continually provide our members with quality goods and services at the lowest possible prices.

As Costco's original executive team set out to implement this mission, we each knew where we fit in.

When we set out to decide on what electronics to stock in our warehouses, we didn't follow the path of other discount retailers who sold marginal off-brand items. We were committed to selling the best-quality products we could, so every decision we made was built around the idea that quality was important.

As the *New York Times* recently noted, the Costco formula combined high quality with "stunningly low prices." And we were truly committed to sell at the best-prices possible. When we sold a commodity product like sugar, for example, we would literally pull it off the shelf for awhile if a local supermarket was using it as a loss leader and selling it below cost. We couldn't match the price and we would never sell below cost. We wanted our customers to be confident that the products they bought at Costco were, indeed, at the lowest possible price.

Costco's success was due, in no small part, to our laser-like single-minded focus on our corporate mission.

That's why from the very start of the Washington Education Foundation we've maintained a sharp focus on our mission.

There are plenty of important things that we could do for kids. And there are plenty of alternative mission statements that might make sense for an organization such as ours.

For example, consider how different we'd be if our mission statement was this instead:

We provide high-achieving students with opportunities to further their lives and careers.

That would be a perfectly good mission statement for an organization that wants to support many of the same children that we do. But the decisions that might be made would likely be quite different.

At the Washington Education Foundation, for example, we

believe that attending a four-year university and receiving a bachelor's degree is the best way for our children to prepare themselves for the future. Certainly, the community college structure provides an excellent transition for many young people. But as noted earlier, we've seen all too many kids stop their education after starting a two-year program, and sometimes they don't even complete their AA degree.

But even more critical is the fact that many *low-income kids* who have the *high potential* to succeed in a four-year college setting are forced into community colleges due to a lack of financial support and resources. We think that's wrong—which is why our mission highlights the importance of getting these kids into a four-year university or college right out of high school whenever possible.

Our mission includes the important aspect of *mentoring*, which we believe is the ideal way to help many high school students make the transition through the first couple of years of college—much better for many kids than forcing them to go it alone.

As you can see, the *opportunities* mission statement would essentially suggest a series of decisions based on the idea that these students are able to go it alone. Essentially, the organization could just give the money and run, counting on the students to make their own

> Only 6 percent of students from the lowest-income families earn bachelor's degrees within five years of completing high school, compared to 41 percent from the highest-income families.

opportunities once they have their scholarships in hand. Some of our students have demonstrated that they would certainly be capable of doing that—especially the ones who have already had to work long hours and played a major part in keeping their families afloat. But all too many lack the background, the knowledge, and the resources to succeed, and even the most capable would likely find the first two years of college to be particularly challenging.

We have more to say—much more—about the importance of

mentoring throughout this book. About why mentoring needs to start early, in the middle and high school years, when students are first beginning to make decisions about college, decisions that will affect their entire lives.

Two-Year Plan

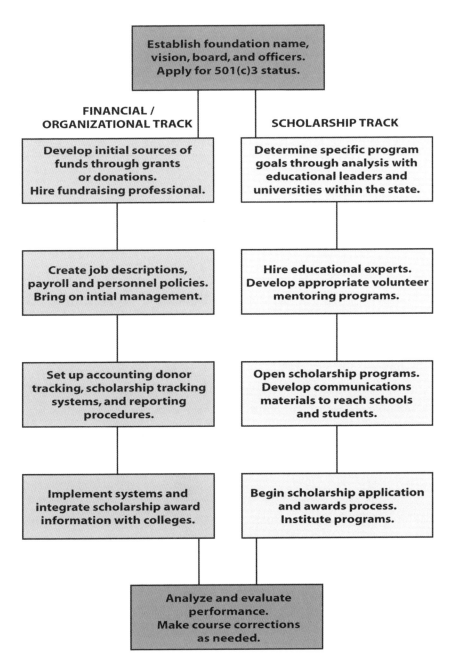

While every foundation will have somewhat different goals and face varying challenges, the Two-Year Plan chart is designed to provide a blueprint for success. Your roadmap will surely look somewhat different but this one, we hope, will give you a good place to start.

4

CREATE CHANGE

THE THEORY OF CHANGE

The goal of the Washington Education Foundation is to contribute to the elimination of income disparity and racial inequality by increasing the number of bachelor's degrees attained by low-income students.

By helping these students earn bachelor's degrees, we believe over time that we can help to break the cycle of poverty, allowing these smart and talented young people to participate successfully in the modern American economy and to make outstanding contributions to society. We all win.

At the Washington Education Foundation we've come up with a multi-pronged approach to how we plan and implement scholarship programs. It is, to be honest, somewhat different from how people viewed scholarships in the past—typically with a focus on rewarding students based solely on cognitive measures which could be identified and tested in traditional ways. Instead, in order to break the cycle of poverty and hopelessness that befalls so many young people, we decided to approach the problem in non-traditional ways, and to make that perspective a fundamental part of how we would come to solutions.

To accomplish this, the Foundation has implemented a Theory of Change—a model for building a strong multi-sector partnership committed to the goal of increasing the number of bachelor's degrees received by students in our state, by decreasing the number of kids left behind.

To be sure, our Theory of Change represents a different way of looking at how to solve the problems of education and of society. An essential element in that Theory is creating a public–private partnership that can work together for the benefit of both, led by a series of "champions"—including leaders within the Foundation—benefactors within the private sector who are willing to donate money and/or time, and key representatives of government at both the state and federal levels.

This public–private partnership is another non-traditional way we approach the issue. We recognize that government has limited resources, and while we consider education central and essential to the government's role, we also know that limited dollars will limit what can be done for students. And what's more, the problem will only get worse as the cost of education continues to skyrocket and the amount of public money available for scholarships stays flat or—even worse—decreases.

At the same time, we feel the public sector plays an essential role as a catalyst and a guiding force in making decisions about education, one that can be augmented through private contributions and activities, but not replaced.

The process works best, we feel, as a public–private partnership, with the public and private sectors each contributing what it does best. At the Washington Education Foundation, for example, we've always received outstanding support (as I'll describe in Chapter 7) from the staff of the Higher Education Coordinating Board (HECB), which is charged with administering all the state's financial aid programs for students. They live with issues related to education every day; they have a long record of working closely with students

Washington Education Foundation's Theory of Change

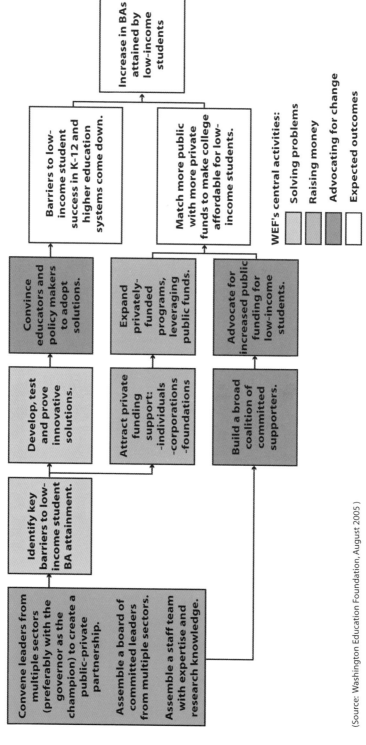

WEF's central activities:

Solving problems

Raising money

Advocating for change

Expected outcomes

(Source: Washington Education Foundation, August 2005)

and of understanding the needs of students in our state.

As we defined what we were going to do with the Foundation, members of the HECB worked closely with us, both to help us understand the complexities of the problems as well as to suggest how we might most effectively organize our scholarship programs in order to craft solutions.

That way, when other organizations came forward with offers to help, the framework of what we were going to do was already in place. Private organizations and individuals could feel confident that their contributions would produce the maximum benefit and be handled in a manner that was consistent with other public activities. This is, in essence, a blueprint that not only reflects how we did things in Washington state, but also how other states might go about creating and implementing successful scholarship programs.

The preliminary stage in implementing the Theory of Change is bringing together several key individuals with a vested stake in improving the educational status of low-income students in the state. Ideally this would include the state governor along with a group of committed leaders from multiple sectors, including college-access experts, to discuss opportunities on the many ways to address the problems and challenges confronting low-income students. Together, these groups should seek to develop a partnership to address the barriers to students within the state that can keep them from attending college and ultimately attaining bachelor's degrees.

The initial convening group of leaders should include:

- The governor and senior government representatives, from both state and local levels
- Key figures, including CEOs and senior managers from businesses in the state
- Leaders and staff members from leading foundations, particularly ones that have an interest in educational and socio-economic issues

- Leaders from academia including university presidents, heads of admissions departments, and other education experts
- Concerned community citizens and other committed individuals

This initial group would identify the barriers to low-income students. Together as a group, they should commit to implementing solutions and bringing new resources to the challenge. Ideally, the Governor would become a major advocate for the effort, and be prepared both to support the effort publicly as well as to provide additional key contacts.

The convening of this group represents the genesis of a multi-sector partnership, a State Education Foundation, with a strong multi-sector board and an expert staff focused on:

- **Solving problems:** This process involves identifying key barriers to low-income students receiving degrees, and then testing and proving what kinds of innovative solutions will best serve the particular needs of the students in each particular state.
- **Raising money:** Effective fundraising means attracting private funding to support scholarships, infrastructure, and research and development, demonstrating innovative solutions to leverage success by attracting mutually reinforcing and sustainable funding from broad-based private sector supporters matched by the state and federal governments.
- **Advocating for change:** The Foundation can become a public voice for change in college access for low-income students, working with state constituent groups to expand adoption of Foundation solutions to increase funding for programs and financial aid that support

low-income students as they work toward their bachelor's degrees.

None of this can happen, of course, without a strong Board made up of leading members of the business, civic and educational communities. In my view, it's important to get all three.

- **Business leaders** are not only able to help provide guidance that can efficiently and effectively shape the organization, they are also in a strong position to make suggestions about how to oversee the organization's daily management decisions. Business leaders can represent a challenge as well, however, since the job of running a private foundation is typically quite different from running a publicly traded corporation. To find the right people, you need to be sure you've identified business leaders who are willing to commit their time and their energy—not always easy, to be honest, when they have plenty of their own business concerns to attend to—and who are also prepared to listen and learn from educational and other professionals, rather than always wanting to run the show themselves.
- **Community-minded civic leaders** provide essential contacts and serve an all-important role as cheerleaders— the ones who can keep the flame alive even when it appears to be flickering. Perhaps one of the hardest things to do in any organization is to keep people excited about the cause once they've moved beyond the initial flush of enthusiasm. The community-minded leaders are the ones who can keep your Board charged and enthused about the important work at hand.
- It may seem obvious to suggest that you should include **educational experts** on your Board, but what's not so

obvious is how their talents can best be utilized. Most important, educational experts provide a reality check for your Board, bringing to the table the culmination of their first-hand experiences with other programs that have been successful (or not). Sometimes, they may serve to dampen enthusiasm—appropriately, when the goals of the Board are trying to reach too far beyond what realistically can be accomplished. They also serve as a conduit into how educational institutions in your state really work, allowing you to pinpoint the key people in each institution that will make it possible to get things done—such as those who can establish mentoring programs and monitor student progress on an ongoing basis.

We'll talk at more length about staffing the organization in Chapter 9, but the important thing to remember here—as shown in the chart at the beginning of this chapter—is that your staff team needs to have the expertise and the ability to research so that your foundation can work effectively.

What team members need to do—what, in fact, is the first charter of all of these groups—is to identify what the key barriers to success are for the students in your state. We've identified many of them in earlier chapters, but the specifics in your state may vary somewhat from the situation in Washington state. For example, while language and cultural differences can represent challenges everywhere, this may be a bigger or smaller factor based on the demographic profile of your students. What's more, the key driving factors can change over time, based on economic and social fluctuations, so you need to maintain flexibility in your programs so that these changes can be addressed.

Once you've identified the barriers, it's time to go to work on solutions. It's important that you look for innovative approaches to scholarship programs, but it's just as important that you test and challenge those approaches so that you know that what you're doing is effective. To do this, you'll need to convince educators and policymakers to adopt specific solutions—and they'll understandably want some proof before committing time and money. What's more, the only way you can really craft good solutions is to allow them to evolve over time, fine-tuning those innovative ideas in a way that allows you to do the best possible job.

For example, at the Washington Education Foundation we've always felt that mentors could play a key role in supporting students—which we think is one of our most important innovations—but the exact nature of that role has evolved from

Identify what the key barriers to success are for the students in your state.

when we started. For example, we realize that we needed to establish a structure to monitor mentors in the same way the mentors monitor students, in order to ensure that everything is running smoothly—from having the right training for advising students effectively, to just making it to meetings, and to feeling rewarded for the hard work they have accepted on a volunteer basis. We've continued to improve our mentoring program year after year, which is one reason I think we've continued to see improvements in the retention and graduation rates of students.

Simultaneously with these program development efforts, our Theory of Change also suggests that you need to actively pursue funds on an ongoing basis and continue to work on building a broad coalition of supporters who can advocate for increased public funding for low-income students. This is a continuous job, not just a one-shot effort up front. Recognize that some percentage of your early advocates are not going to be with you over the long haul, either due to changing personal conditions, government elections, or other interests or concerns that may come to the forefront for them and take them away. Plus, like any good organization your

Chris Wells
Château Ste. Michelle Scholar

OPPORTUNITY WITHOUT BURDEN

"Thanks to my scholarship," notes Chris Wells, "I was able to have the opportunity to focus on my studies and complete my undergraduate work without the financial burdens of college."

Since Chris's freshman year, the average cost of attending a four-year university rose more than 20 percent (with all the evidence suggesting that it will continue to rise for years to come). Between scholarships, summer work, internships, and parental support, Chris was able to accomplish something that nobody in his family before him had done: graduate from college. His parents had always emphasized the importance of education to him, as well as the importance of excelling in school.

"I came from a strong household," he says, "and I was very involved in sports during high school, quarterbacking for O'Dea. My parents always said to give my all to everything I did. I knew I was going to attend college—even without a scholarship, I probably would have still attended. But I would have had to work my way through school, and I wouldn't have been able to get involved in as many student activities or achieve the same level of grades."

In fact, Chris earned better grades in college than in high school, graduating in June 2005 from Washington State University with a 3.3 grade point average. In addition, the fact that he didn't have to work at a regular job while attending school also meant that he had the opportunity to work in the school's business and diversity programs, mentoring other students and helping them succeed in college. What's more, he was able to network as a business major and prepare himself for career opportunities ahead.

Now that he has graduated—and done it in four years—Chris discovered that a degree quickly opens doors of employment for him. He received job offers from several solid companies upon graduation, and started work in the Human Resources Department at Microsoft shortly after earning his degree.

"Scholarships can level the playing field for everybody," Chris remarks, "and I'm particularly thankful to Mr. Ted Baseler, the President of Château Ste. Michelle, and the rest of the people in that organization for their foresight and commitment to investing in the future of men and women who are striving to change their lives with a university education. I look forward to reaching the point in my career where I have the opportunity to do the same, making an investment in someone else's future."

foundation should seek steady growth that will allow it to continue to be increasingly effective in how it serves the students of your state. If yours is like most organizations, you'll need to start somewhat small, initially able to serve only a portion of the students who could benefit from your help, and then grow over time to serve a larger student population.

What's more, as your foundation becomes established, it can potentially become a leading advocate for education as well, not just at the upper high school and college levels, but in K–12 as well as pre-school educational efforts.

These efforts take time, and to be honest you'll probably always have more to do and more students who could be helped by your support. But in time, your efforts can help to bring down the educational barriers confronted by low-income students while making education more affordable for those students. The result is that more of these students in need will receive their bachelor's degrees and some percentage will attain advanced degrees as well.

This Theory of Change will therefore, we believe, have a positive impact throughout society, resulting in far-reaching changes.

From its inception, the Washington Education Foundation has sought to provide a sustainable reduction in barriers that low-income students face across the entire educational system by proving that solutions are already at hand through its own initiatives in high schools and colleges, and then advocating for change within the K–12 and higher education system. The Foundation has aspired to have each of its solutions integrated into the public system over time, thus providing opportunities to all low-income students, not just those in locations where programs already exist.

Similarly, we have sought to develop sustained increases in available funding to make college affordable for low-income students, bringing both private and public resources to bear in order to increase funding. Through our own fund development activities, we've sought to expand private funding of scholarships and programs by reaching out to Washington's business sector, foundations, community associations and individuals to build a sustained funding stream for low-income student scholarships.

As former Lutheran missionary Dr. William Foege recently noted with a chuckle in the *Seattle Post-Intelligencer,* "People tend to underestimate the amount of altruism that exists among some who work in corporations, just as they underestimate the amount of greed among churchworkers, civil servants, and government employees."

Through advocacy, we have sought public matching for the private funds and increased commitments to student financial aid at the state and federal levels.

The combined effect of the reduction in barriers for all low-income students and the increase in funds from both the private and public sectors has helped to put us well on the road to achieving the Foundation's ultimate goal—that no student be ignored nor left behind.

5

CHAMPIONS

FINDING EXECUTIVE CHAMPIONS

To deliver on the promises that are implicit in the Theory of Change, we believe that it's essential to find leaders for your foundation who are committed both to the cause of education as well as to the broader business and social needs of the community.

This is no small task. While there may be people willing to commit some of their time to a Foundation, it's essential to identify people with both the right contacts and the right commitment that will allow them to get the job done.

While there are surely cases in which a single individual can serve as the leader, in our experience with the Washington Education Foundation we recommend that you identify *two* people to serve as champions. Sometimes, frankly, the work can be overwhelming, even when you're in the process of collecting initial donations and defining your original programs. And as the foundation develops, it can become an even bigger and bigger challenge, especially as you take on the management of staff, the detailed definition and development of scholarship opportunities, the implementation of programs, and the measuring of results—all while you still have to bang the drum loudly and serve as an advocate for education among people in both the public sector and the private sector. If you have two people who are committed, the work of guiding the foundation—while still a huge responsibility—can be somewhat less daunting.

The two champions you select to manage the efforts of the Foundation should share a passion to try to help these students navigate through a four-year baccalaureate program. It's important that these champions:

- Be community-minded and committed to service
- Know "who's who" in the world of charitable giving
- Be able to communicate well with the higher-ed community, including university presidents, faculties, administrations, and staffs

Most importantly, these two people do have to be responsible for fundraising. The champions need to be the people who get out into the community and represent the face and the vision of the foundation. What's more, they have to oversee the revenue streams for the foundation, both in terms of scholarship and administration.

This isn't something you can delegate to a middle-management person, especially as you're kicking off your organization. As soon as you do that, it typically becomes wrapped up in process, and limits your ability to communicate your vision to the right people, especially people of means or the kinds of foundations that have huge amounts of resources to really make a difference in the community.

Furthermore, these champions need to be politically savvy so they can talk to the federal Department of Education as well as to state government, and communicate what they are trying to accomplish. Once again, we would emphasize that the champions must have a good working relationship with the Governor of the state, because a Governor brings significant clout to the operation— a Governor's Rolodex alone is a terrific resource for communicating to a lot of essential, influential people.

There's a tremendous opportunity for the champions in working with the college presidents, trustees, and boards of regents. Obviously we're all in this thing for the same reason and that is to help the children of the state attain the highest level of education they're capable of achieving, by coming up with the resources to do that, and then ensuring that they're getting the mentoring they need to be successful.

> A high school senior anywhere in this great land of ours can apply to any college or any university in any of the 50 states and not be turned away because his family is poor.
>
> -Lyndon B. Johnson

This is all well and good, but it can't overshadow the basic notion that we are in the business of helping financially disadvantaged children who, without our assistance, wouldn't be able to earn their baccalaureate degrees. In 1965, President Lyndon B. Johnson made a simple promise to low-income students that "A high school senior anywhere in this great land of ours can apply to any college or any university in any of the 50 states and not be turned away because his family is poor." That has to be your light and the inspiration for your champions.

As I've always told people—if we can help one kid, that's great. Help a hundred, that's better. A thousand is terrific, 10,000 is unbelievable and, of course, remember the goal is 40,000! But it's not a matter of quantity as it is a concern about quality. That's the overriding responsibility of the champions. Once they're in place and have established the vision for the organization, everything begins to make sense.

But that's just the beginning.

After setting the direction for the foundation, these champions need to identify the individuals who will lead and manage the everyday work of the organization.

Some champions may choose to do this themselves, but I would recommend against it. Think of it as similar to the relationship between a Chair of the Board and the Chief Executive Officer. The Chair has ultimate responsibility for the organization and should be well acquainted with most of the details of how it's run. But the Chair really has more of an oversight role.

The Chief Executive Officer, by comparison, manages the day-to-day operations of a company. CEOs focus on the hiring of staff, the development of systems, and the hundreds of details implicit in the creation of new products and programs.

Coming back to the foundation world, the champions may give shape to the organization and help to continually refine the vision. But it's best if much of their energy can be spent reaching out to the community and serving that public role as an educational advocate. Like a corporate chair, the foundation champions should regularly review the organization's financial position and performance but the champions should, in the majority of cases, leave most of the decisions to the people they select.

I know this isn't an absolute model. Every foundation will need to find what works best. At the same time, I think there can be multiple problems when the visionaries who create the foundation try to micromanage every aspect of it. Instead, hire the right people and let them do that job! And then continue hiring the right people to help you grow the organization.

While doing this you need to be continually learning. Every day you need to learn how to do something better—a new idea—or improvise on an old idea and elevate the performance of your entire operation.

Let me take a moment and tell you about Ann Ramsay-Jenkins, who as noted earlier is the co-founder of the Washington Education Foundation and, as such, the champion who really sparked our organization right from the start.

Even before we developed the Foundation, Ann already had a stellar background and was a notable leader in the community. For example, she had chaired the United Way Board in 1995, at which time she saw first-hand the kinds of tragedies that can befall young people. She also served as Chair of the Seattle Repertory Theater Foundation, helping them work through the challenges of raising money and raising awareness beyond the arts community.

Her professional experience includes a five-year stint as Director of the Office of Budgets at Harvard University, as Assistant Secretary of Administration & Finance for the Commonwealth of Massachusetts, and as a Management Associate in the Office of Management & Budget, Executive Office of the President, in Washington, DC. Ann was appointed a White House Fellow in 1972 and served in the Executive Office of the President, Office of Drug Abuse Prevention, where she received the Distinguished Service Award in 1973. She also served as a board member of the Institute of Politics at the Kennedy School of Government at Harvard University and as a member of President Carter's Advisory Committee for Women.

Ann has a special knack for getting people excited—really excited—about supporting compassionate causes. Ann has always had a deep social conscience and demonstrates her concerns both on an individual level as well as a broad social level. I remember her saying early on: "How do you eliminate poverty? One scholarship at a time."

Working as a team, Ann and I have been able not only to bring shape to the Washington Education Foundation, but we have been able to bounce ideas off each other and utilize our individual skills in the most effective way.

With both of us working diligently, the Foundation has grown quickly. Looking forward, we have such an outstanding staff that we can focus our efforts on what we do best: raising awareness of the needs, keeping the vision alive and, of course, raising money.

I̲t̲ T̲akes a C̲hampion. . .

Champions come in all shapes and sizes and from all walks of life. But they all share certain common attributes:

- **It takes courage to be a champion.**
  It takes the courage to stand up and be counted for what you believe. The courage to face adversity and sometimes, the criticisms of others. The courage to stick with your dreams and your plans, even when it might be simply easier to give up.

- **It takes focus and commitment to be a champion.**
  You need focus to determine where you can have the greatest impact. You need to commit to deliver your time and resources, year after year, so that the impact generated by your contributions can flourish and grow.

- **It takes passion and vision to be a champion.**
  Passion is required to relentlessly pursue your goals, and you need vision to see how those pursuits can make the world a better place.

- **It takes hard work to be a champion.**
  That means the kind of hard work in which you literally have to create something out of nothing and then stick to your goals and get the job done, year after year.

- **It takes a dream to be a champion.**
  We need to stick to the dream of how each of us can do our part to make the world a better place.

On the following pages, you'll meet some of the champions who have made a difference in the world of education.

The Three Doctors

It takes courage to be a champion. The courage to stand up and be counted for what you believe. The courage to face adversity, and sometimes the criticisms, of others. The courage to stick with your dreams and your plans, even when it might be easier simply to give up.

The Three Doctors—Dr. Sampson Davis, Dr. George Jenkins, and Dr. Rameck Hunt—have needed a lot of courage in their lives. Raised in the poorest corner of Newark, New Jersey, they developed a friendship at a young age that was destined to change their lives and the lives of tens of thousands of other people around the country.

Life wasn't easy for them—they grew up without their fathers around for most of their young lives, with drugs and violence an everyday reality for them, even sometimes at home. At times, the temptations of the streets offered such allure that they stepped onto the wrong side of the law, though they managed to correct themselves and eventually get their lives in order.

In high school, the three of them made a pact—an agreement to share a dream together, which must have seemed like nothing more than a fantasy at the time. That dream was to beat the streets, go to medical school, and become doctors.

The dream started in an unlikely way, with three friends skipping class, ostensibly to hear a presentation about Seton Hall University in the school library. Their real plan, typical of 11th graders, was to go shoot baskets instead.

Fortunately (though they didn't feel that way at the time), the school principal caught them on their way to the gym and re-directed them back to the library. They slid into seats at a back table of the room, figuring they were stuck listening to a boring presentation.

George was the first to get enthused. At age 11, he had gotten braces through an outreach program at the University of Medicine and Dentistry in New Jersey. It sowed the seeds of his dream, to become a dentist some day—not that he really thought he had much hope of affording college and dental school. Today, incidentally, Dr. Jenkins has not only accomplished his dream, but he's also in charge of that same outreach program, serving kids in the community in the same way he was once served.

It was George who first suggested they form a pact, and all become doctors together. While Sam and Rameck had some glimmer of hope to attend college, their plans were nebulous. Sam hoped he could play college baseball somewhere; Rameck thought he might attend Howard. The idea of committing not only to four years of college, but to additional years of professional training, seemed almost inconceivable at the time.

But they figured that they had nothing to lose by applying to the Seton Hall program, and if they did somehow manage to be accepted, the education would be free.

They were right. College presented its hard moments, and sometimes they came close to getting into trouble once again. But they survived with the help of educational mentors and counselors and, most especially, with the help of each other. After completing their professional training, all three later reached their goal of becoming doctors.

If that were where the story ended, it would already be amazing.

But in a sense, that's nothing more than just the beginning of the story. Because while they had never imagined their pact would last beyond their educational years, it has. The Three Doctors kept their pact together to tell their story and to work to help others like them in their community, and even across the country, to turn their lives around.

Dr. Davis is not only a board certified emergency medical physician but he also participates in the Violence Prevention Institute, showing real-life footage of the emergency room effects of street violence to grammar school kids to offset the sometimes-romanticized images that are prevalent among young people.

Dr. Hunt is a board certified internist at University Medical Center at Princeton and Clinical Assistant Professor of Medicine at Robert Wood Johnson Medical School.

And Dr. Jenkins, as noted, is both a dentist and a teacher, not only reaching out to people who can't afford dental care, but working closely with promising disadvantaged students to foster their education.

Together, they've formed the Three Doctors Foundation, which offers health, mentoring, and scholarship support to those who can't afford it. They spend countless hours helping to steer young people down a positive path and serving as role models of what education can mean to a person.

"We want education to have the same mass appeal to young people as music and sports," says Dr. Davis. "But to do that, young people need to see faces. Today, it's the face of the Three Doctors. Maybe some day it'll be the Four Engineers, the Five Teachers, and the Six CEOs."

Oprah Winfrey has called them the "premier role models in America," and they have received the *Essence* Lifetime Achievement Award.

Quite simply, they are amazing in how they interact with young people—and I saw this first-hand when they spoke at a recent Costco fundraising breakfast and follow-up student session.

But really, when you think about it, they're role models for all of us, inspiring us to realize that we can do more, and do better, to contribute to our communities.

"We've witnessed that dual mode in role modeling," agrees Dr. Hunt. "Sure, we're role models for the kids; we connect with them because we come from similar neighborhoods and similar backgrounds. We can talk to them in a language they understand, from a shared culture.

"But we also have seen that what we're doing has helped encourage other professionals to self-reflect. Too many people get sidetracked in their lives. The stuff we're doing reminds people that there's always time, and always a way, to give back."

The key to their success?

"In everything we're doing—in the professional arena, in what we're doing to help out," says Dr. Jenkins, "we're following our hearts."

To find out more about the outstanding work of the Three Doctors, visit the website for their foundation at *www.threedoctorsfoundation.org.* Their story is told in greater detail in *The Pact,* their first book, which follows the story of their struggles and rise to success and in *We Beat the Street,* which tells the same story but in a style designed to reach out specifically to the young people that may be facing some of the same struggles that they did.

Costco Executive Team

It takes focus and commitment to be a champion. We all need focus to determine where each of us can have the greatest impact. Commitment is required to deliver your time and resources, year after year, so that the impact generated by your contributions can flourish and grow.

Unlike some other companies, Costco has always taken a relatively low-key approach to its donation programs. While the company gives generously—both through its corporate gifts and executive employee matching programs—it has made these donations out of a genuine sense of corporate responsibility and not for public relations purposes. What's more, Costco gives of its time as well as its money. The culture of the company has long encouraged volunteerism and in communities across the country, Costco employees are active volunteers in roles that range from tutoring and mentoring students to taking Board positions in volunteer organizations.

Costco Chairman Jeff Brotman comments, "Over a period of 20 years of being active in our communities and giving away money, we've never promoted ourselves as philanthropists—both as a corporation and in our personal giving. However, people do figure it out and reflect on it, which I believe reflects back on the company in a positive way.

"This is enlightened self-interest. The more you do for people, the more you bring them into the business, the more you understand their cultures and needs, and the more you will succeed."

"Giving money intelligently is one of the most difficult things to do," observes Costco President and CEO Jim Sinegal. "We think hard about every donation we make to ensure it can make a real difference."

It's the same way Costco operates its business. A *New York Times* article noted that Costco's average pay for workers is 42 percent higher than its competitor, Sam's Club, and that they also offered health policies that "make other retailers look Scroogish."

"This is good business," Jim explains, noting that good wages and good benefits are why Costco has such low employee turnover and low theft rates.

Historically, the parameters defining the company's donations have been concentrated in those areas in which they can do the most good—focusing on health, human services and education. For example, Costco has not only consistently made donations through the United Way, but has also supported Children's hospitals in Seattle as well as in other states and provinces.

In addition, for two decades, Costco has helped to sponsor an annual breakfast for Zion Academy, a pre-school to grade eight private inner-city school supporting African-American children. The reason? A deep and abiding belief in the importance of education;

especially, a conviction that education can be a strong force for changing the world.

"Young children are enthusiastic about learning," observes Jim. "We want to help encourage that enthusiasm. Unfortunately, I sometimes feel that without good programs in their schools, all too many children lose that enthusiasm by 3rd grade—and then they never get it back."

In 1998, Initiative 200 passed in the state of Washington. Modeled after a similar California initiative, it made it impossible for universities to actively recruit minority students as they had in the past.

"We couldn't turn our back on the situation," notes Jim. "We felt we had to act."

Jim, Jeff, and the rest of the executive team decided they were in a good position to make a difference. As noted by Dick DiCerchio, Senior Executive Vice President and COO, "The only thing that most of these students needed was an opportunity to go to college. Often, their lives are teetering on the edge—but education can change their lives, the lives of their families, and the health of our community."

Building on its experience with the Zion breakfast, the Costco team decided to sponsor an annual breakfast to provide scholarships for minority students to attend the University of Washington and Seattle University.

While these executives prefer a low-key approach to giving, they felt this issue was important enough that they had to step forward and take a more visible leadership role rather than working behind the scenes as they had done before. They decided to demonstrate their commitment to the cause in a way that would encourage others in the business community to follow their example.

The breakfast has been a rousing success—raising $1.2 million the first year and more than $10 million over six years. That translates into more than 500 students that have been able to attend these universities—providing not only a great education for those

Charisse Arce
Costco Scholar

It Takes a Village. . .

There are more people living in Charisse Arce's college dormitory than in her village.

A native of Alaska, Charisse comes from Iliamna, a tundra town of 250 people. To an outsider, the town doesn't look like it offers much, but to the people who live there it has everything: eagles, moose, porcupines, cranberries, salmonberries, and the Northern Lights. The traditions in the villages are strong: listening to elders' stories, caribou hunting, and fishing in weather so cold you can actually become stuck in the ice.

To most people in Iliamna, Alaska and the surrounding villages, high school graduation is the end of academic learning. This fact is a shame. While the traditions of village life are wonderful, all too many young people with great potential waste away, not recognizing great talents that could have been developed if only they had the opportunity to go to college.

Some of them, no doubt, would return to the village after graduation, able to contribute to its leadership and ongoing needs in health, education, and other fields.

Thanks to a Costco Scholarship, Charisse was among the first students to benefit from a college education, attending Seattle University. "Attending college has opened me up to so much," she says, "including communicating with people from different backgrounds and points of view. I have come to appreciate that I can be a proud Alaskan Native and be part of a greater global community."

At Seattle University, Charisse has served as a mentor for minority freshmen and as an officer for the Native American Club. Back home, she's able to spend time with other students who are in the same position that she was, helping to motivate them to think about the possibility of attending college.

In one sense, not a lot has really changed—Charisse still looks forward to going home, eating her mom's caribou soup, and enjoying the company of her family. But thanks to young people like Charisse and other recipients of the Costco Scholarship fund, everything has changed, because an entire new world of opportunity and hope has opened up for them.

students, but having a significant impact on the diversity at each campus as well.

The breakfast brings together a collection of community leaders, benefactors, Costco suppliers, and others. The event has featured notable speakers, including The Three Doctors, highlighted earlier in this book. This year, Lieutenant Colonel (Retired) Consuelo Kickbusch, who overcame poverty to become the highest-ranking Hispanic woman in the Combat Support field of the United States Army, gave an inspiring speech about her career and the importance of education.

But the real highlight of the event is the students—both the student speakers, who tell amazing stories of their lives and how the scholarships have helped them, as well as the other scholarship participants who sit at each table and share their personal accounts.

"It would be a sin if these kids had fallen through the cracks for lack of a scholarship," notes Dick. "We're pleased with the impact we've been able to have on their lives."

The Bill & Melinda Gates Foundation

It takes passion and vision to be a champion. It takes passion to relentlessly pursue your goals, and vision to see how those pursuits can make the world a better place.

"Our dream at the Bill & Melinda Gates Foundation," notes Bill Gates Sr., "is to help talented students achieve their dreams.

"But," he notes, "there's a hole in our society. The biggest problem with many programs that are meant to do good is that the people who choose to participate are the ones who need it the least. And the ones who need the most help don't show up."

That's why the Gates Foundation has crafted a different sort of model for the causes it supports around the world, including education. For example, they don't just dole out checks to schools and then sit on the sidelines hoping for the best. Instead, they get actively involved helping to shape the schools, and then in analyzing the results of their programs. They make sure that the people who need the help are the ones most likely to get it.

In the case of education, Bill Gates Sr. believes strongly that helping to pay for a student's education isn't enough. Each student has to be prepared for college and supported so that they have the best chance to succeed.

"Our public education system continues to steer children of color away from college preparatory classes and away from college," he notes. "Our belief is that nothing will fundamentally change unless we change how students are taught."

It's a model of philanthropy that hearkens back to the era of the Carnegie endowments, in which successful business and professional people work hand-in-hand, rather than at arm's length.

Still, Mr. Gates Sr. is remarkably humble, and prefers to work behind the scenes. He isn't really interested in bringing a lot of attention to himself, but he is interested in bringing more attention to the needs of education at every level—from scholarship programs such as ours all the way to the early-learning initiatives that the Bill & Melinda Gates Foundation is currently exploring and implementing.

Bill Gates Sr. had an outstanding career as a successful and prominent attorney, as well as a trustee, officer, and volunteer for more than two dozen Northwest organizations.

As noted earlier in this book, he was instrumental in helping to shape and support the Washington Education Foundation, right from the start. I think of him as my mentor. Because of his passion and vision for education, he got involved in some of our earliest conversations with business and political leaders across the state. He helped to define how we could best support students and how that support could be integrated with other efforts of the Gates Foundation.

To be honest, the Gates Foundation didn't always say yes to everything we wanted. And when they did say yes, they made it clear that they expected the highest performance in terms of both objectives and results.

"My son comes from the business world," Bill Gates Sr. observes. "He and his wife don't feel that everything they have belongs to them alone. But he likes good investments and feels that investing in education is important."

Recently, Mr. Gates Sr. spoke to the more than 500 scholars who participated in the Washington Education Foundation's summer Achievers College Experience (ACE) program, in which the scholarship recipients spend a week experiencing life on a college campus and learn how best to apply themselves during their senior year in high school.

"As you go through life, you'll face challenges and opportunities every day," Mr. Gates told the participants. "But as you face them, you should ask yourself three questions: Can you be trusted? Do you do the most-important things first? And are you prepared to share with others—not just money, but your time and energy as well.

"You can make the world a better place," he continues, "and beginning with college, enjoy the most marvelous experience of your life as well."

Dr. Deborah Wilds

It takes a lifetime of hard work to be a champion. It takes the kind of hard work in which you literally have to create something out of nothing, and then stick to your goals and get the job done, year after year.

In one sense, it's no surprise that Deborah Wilds committed her life to education at an early age.

Her mother was trained as a teacher and passed on her respect for the essential importance of education to her daughter.

Still, her father didn't have the benefits even of a high school education, dropping out of school after eighth grade, which might be one reason Dr. Wilds developed a different perspective on education from a very early age. She realized that the current system wasn't doing nearly enough to enable young people to finish high school ready for college and to be successful when they got there.

> A lot of young people who never even imagined themselves in college are graduating with degrees in disciplines that range from science to marketing to psychology.

She recalls that other than her family she wasn't encouraged to attend college—hardly anyone in the educational system told her what she needed to do—from selecting the right college preparatory courses to making the right choices as she considered and applied for colleges.

She committed her life to changing all that—changing, for example, not only the hopes and aspirations of young people, but also the expectations and beliefs of the adults in schools who advise them. Changing the very structure of the schools themselves, solving the problems that result when schools get too large and impersonal, which too often results in kids falling through the cracks.

Dr. Wilds' dedication to improving educational outcomes for children of color and poor children reflects her deeply held belief that as our nation becomes more technologically advanced and dependent on the intellectual capital of its citizens, the need to expand educational opportunities within underserved communities becomes even more pronounced.

At the Bill & Melinda Gates Foundation, Dr. Wilds has been a leading advocate for shaping education in a way that can change not only the lives of students, but society as a whole. But to really succeed at that, she and the other champions at the Foundation have focused on a lot of fundamental questions about how education works—smaller schools, higher expectations of achievement, and more rigor in evaluating results.

Judging from the reactions and the achievements of the students—including several of those profiled in these pages—it's working. A lot of young people who never even imagined themselves in college are graduating with degrees in disciplines that range from science to marketing to psychology.

But it's just a first step. As Dr. Wilds points out, we need to do more to support the teachers, and we need to do more to make all kids winners—not just those who are awarded scholarships. There needs to be, she says, a significant adult in every child's life.

Clearly, her life's work has had a hugely significant impact on the lives of many children.

Ted Baseler

It takes a dream to be a champion. It takes a dream of how each of us can do our part to make the world a better place.

When Ted Baseler became President of Château Ste. Michelle winery (CSM) in 2000, he wanted to carry forward the winery's long-standing tradition of supporting the community.

"A successful business has an obligation to share its success in a way that can make a difference," says Baseler. "We felt that education could be the great equalizer and that supporting education would be a way in which, through a scholarship program, our company could make a difference."

What's more, because of its highly diverse workforce, Château Ste. Michelle felt it could make a unique contribution by focusing on diversity, especially in light of the passage of Initiative 200 in Washington state, which limited the ability of public institutions to offer assistance based on cultural factors.

"Our winery owns and operates more than 5,000 acres of vineyards in Washington with more than 900 employees, many of them of Hispanic heritage," notes Baseler. "Many of these workers want their children to have the opportunities they didn't, and be able to attend college. While our scholarships are by no means limited to the families of our employees, we always feel particularly gratified and excited when a CSM scholarship is awarded to the child of a farmworker family."

Funds for the Château Ste. Michelle scholarship are raised through a special dinner concert each year at the winery's grounds in Woodinville, a short drive from Seattle. The winery has operated a summer concert series for years on their grounds, along with numerous charitable events such as an annual auction for Children's Hospital of Seattle, so the scholarship-focused event fit naturally into their other existing programs. Scholarships are awarded to students attending the state's two research institutions: the University of Washington and Washington State University, a first joint fund-raising effort for the two schools.

"We like to say that wine can bring even Huskies and Cougars together!" Baseler remarks. "And we also like to note that with WSU's roots with the wine industry, and the great interest in wine on the UW side of the mountains, this is the perfect place for them to come together."

While celebrating what the scholarship has done to enhance the lives of the young recipients, Baseler notes that there's another, less tangible benefit to giving: "The perception of business among many young people is bad, especially in the wake of recent corporate scandals. By helping society through programs such as this, we hope we can do our part to reach out to young people and change their perspective on business. Many of them, we hope and believe, will become the business leaders of tomorrow."

6

LAST DOLLAR IN

A CRITICAL CONCEPT REGARDING HOW WE HANDLE SCHOLARSHIPS at the Washington Education Foundation is what we call the "last dollar in." What this means is that students collect as many other financial aid opportunities as they can—federal and state grants, work study programs, etc. We then review each student's scholarship situation, determine what the real financial impact on their families and them is likely to be, and then make up the difference—in terms of the last dollars provided into their total pool of funds.

Our goal, in short, is to augment these other grants and scholarship programs, not to replace them.

Sometimes we give more because the information does not really reflect the student's overall situation. For example, while the official formulas sometimes suggest that a family can afford a particular amount of money to support a student through college, some families can't really do that, and some families—such as low-income families who may not always understand the value and the importance of a college education—may not agree to pay.

Similarly, the total scholarship package for an individual student may include elements such as a significant level of student loans that a family might not want the student to pay back. As discussed elsewhere in this book, many of these low-income students have no positive experience with loans in their lives, and if they do take out a loan and don't complete college, they may be worse off than if they hadn't tried to go to college at all, since they need to pay off a large bill without the degree that can help them afford it.

Every case is a little different, though, and we treat every student as an individual when we consider his or her situation.

Our ultimate goal is to maximize educational opportunities for as many students as we can, while using our money most effectively. Thus, in programs such as the Achievers Scholarship Program, every grant we give is a little bit different, and we re-evaluate those grants on a regular basis.

In pure administrative terms, it would be much easier to just give each scholarship recipient a set amount—say, $3,000—rather than trying to customize around the needs of each individual student. For example, you wouldn't have to keep track of the other scholarships each student was receiving nor would you have to monitor students' financial aid situations throughout their time in college.

It would be simpler, but not better. If you give a set grant to every student, you'd quickly discover that many students wouldn't need the full amount of money (although they'd probably come up with a good way of spending it). At the same time, many students would need more, as the scholarship grant would fall short of filling in the gap of what they can afford. The result is that, while giving a standard amount of money might be an easy and efficient way to run an operation, the scholarship money wouldn't really work as hard as it might or serve as many students as it could.

Through the "last dollar in" concept, we are effectively creating a balance between the needs of each student with our desire to genuinely help as many students as we can.

If you're new to this world, here's a bare-bones snapshot of how the scholarship process works (which is admittedly a lot simpler than the real complex situation faced by so many students).

Let's look at a typical list of college expenses at a public university. Costs for each year for a student would work out to something like this:

COSTS

Tuition	$5,000
Fees	500
Books & Supplies	1,000
Room & Board	7,000
Transportation & Personal	<u>1,500</u>
TOTAL	$15,000

All together, a typical annual bill adds up to $15,000. Some students might cost more, especially if they need to travel regularly a long distance to go to school. Some students might need to spend less, especially if they're living at home instead of on campus.

What's more, costs can vary dramatically from one year to the next. A computer science major, for example, almost certainly needs a computer, but he or she doesn't need a new one every year. A student majoring in the arts might, on many campuses, be more easily able to use the public computing facilities provided by the university. Tuition and fees never go down in price, nor do books— the best we can hope is that they remain reasonably stable from one year to the next.

Each year, college students receiving financial aid fill out the FAFSA—the Free Application for Federal Student Aid. This application collects information on the financial situations of students and their families. Sometimes this information can vary dramatically from one year to the next, as family job situations change and as the students themselves may take on part-time work. (If you're interested in getting a more detailed look at how the process works, you can visit the Washington Education Foundation website at *www.waedfoundation.org* and follow our links to the various

scholarship estimators that students can use to get a feel for the
amounts for which they may or may not qualify.)

After completing the FAFSA, an EFC—or Estimated Family
Contribution—is calculated for each student according to standard
formulas. This is simply a guideline on how much the student, along
with his or her family, is expected to contribute to the overall
education.

As you can imagine, the simplicity of the EFC number is fraught
with problems—it's not a bad starting point, but it hardly recognizes
the varied and complex situations of individual students. It is
possible for a student to appeal the decisions based on any changing
circumstances. As with all such appeals, an appeal can be a time-
consuming process and often isn't met with a sympathetic ear.

The information from the FAFSA is then forwarded to the various
colleges in which the student has interest. The colleges look at all
the resources at their disposal—federal Pell Grants, Washington
state Need Grant, and merit and other scholarship opportunities,
along with loans and work-study programs—and put together an
individual package for each student that will be as close as possible
to what the student needs in order to attend.

Many of the people on our staff come from college admission
and scholarship offices, so we're acutely aware of how hard these
schools work to make an education possible. We also work very
closely with them on an ongoing basis, so we know that like us they
want to support as many students as possible, partly because of
their commitment to education but also, quite simply, because these
are great kids who deserve our support and will themselves be able
to contribute so much to society.

At the same time, the schools are themselves trying to work
within limited resources, and have a hard time helping many students
with the kinds of full packages they really need to attend college.
With costs rising, it's hard for them to keep pace or to do as much
as they'd like to do all by themselves.

That's where we come in. The universities provide us with the information on what they are able to offer each of our scholarship recipients. On a case-by-case basis, we evaluate what we can do to make an education possible. Can we reduce or eliminate the loan so that the student will be able to confidently attend college without that burden? We're fans of work-study programs because they not only provide the student with connectivity to the campus but also provide additional mentoring opportunities from the people who are overseeing the student. Still, we always want to be sure that students aren't expected to take on a work-study load that will potentially interfere with their education.

After students have received all the aid they are eligible for, we then award each of them a scholarship that tops off their total need. The following is an example of how this works:

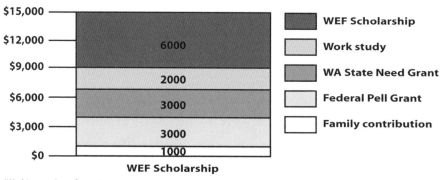

Last Dollar In

(Washington State figures)

7

OUR HEROES—THE BENEFACTORS

ALL THE GOOD INTENTIONS IN THE WORLD ARE MEANINGLESS if you can't raise the money to support students.

But for many people, raising money is the most-difficult part of the process. No one you talk to will ever say they're against supporting education, but getting people to commit actual dollars to the cause is another matter entirely.

To be successful, you have to remember one simple word: *listen*! Listen carefully to what potential benefactors really care about supporting. Are they concerned about the lost potential of students, or the need for more scientists, or the lack of diversity on college campuses, or more structural educational issues, or supporting their alma mater, or are they simply taking on the responsibility of philanthropy?

Listen to whether education is really their focus at all. There is no shortage of deserving causes that compete for the attention of potential benefactors such as healthcare issues like cancer or juvenile diabetes. Arts organizations, in an era of slashed government budgets, depend on community donations for their very existence.

Listen to *how* they want to give—some potential benefactors want more anonymity. These benefactors may want to depend on the recipient organization to manage all the details while others demand and expect to be actively involved at every stage in the process.

It isn't enough to say, "We have all these great kids that deserve your attention." Frankly, there are hundreds of worthy causes that deserve attention. Like any good salesperson, you need to understand what motivates the benefactor, and how the programs you offer can potentially match up with what they want to do.

There won't always be a match. A benefactor who's ready to support one student, for example, doesn't get to reshape all of your donation programs. And a benefactor that might be ready to support hundreds of students doesn't automatically get to define how your smaller donations are handled either.

Instead, there has to be a meeting of the minds, a shared purpose, and a sense that you can work together to accomplish what's important to you both.

The sometimes frustrating part is that you'll probably miss more often than you hit. For every ten calls you make, you may only get one donation—in some situations, you may be lucky to get even that. Plenty of people will say the right things ("Yes, we believe in education" or "Yes, I want to support diversity" and "No, I don't think government is doing enough to support students in need.") but then still not give you a nickel.

The main advice I can give is—don't get discouraged! Rejection is normal in these endeavors. Good intentions do not necessarily translate into good donations.

My other main advice is to trust your instincts, and focus on those people who have genuine interest. Invest the time in them so they can understand how your organization works and how your objectives and theirs merge together.

As noted earlier, at the Washington Education Foundation our approach to programs was highly flexible. We recognized that a Costco or a Gates Foundation would want to be actively involved at every stage in the process—from the definition of the program to the granting of actual scholarships. Other organizations, by comparison, look to us to handle all those details and simply want to feel confident in how we operate and in how their money will be spent.

This point raises another issue: Giving away money costs money. Some percentage of each donation needs to go into program management and to the operational needs of the Foundation itself. Of course, we'd all like to keep these administrative costs as low as possible, and we work hard to ensure that money isn't being spent unnecessarily. At the same time, we recognize that the model we typically recommend, in which a student is supported with mentoring and other tools, costs more in terms of oversight than if we simply gave money away directly.

We think that's the right model, but we also know that we need to clearly explain to potential benefactors why some percentage of their donation—never more than 10 percent—goes into program management. For us, another important element is recognizing that management costs when programs start up are typically higher than when those programs are up and running. We work hard both to accomplish those improved economies of scale and to ensure that our benefactors are aware of that fact.

> We work hard both to accomplish those improved economies of scale and to ensure that our benefactors are aware of that fact.

At the heart of this is the simple truth that credibility of the people heading the Foundation needs to be absolutely solid. And, I would argue, the person who approaches corporations and other organizations for donations needs to have the kind of background and integrity in the community that can open doors to every CEO's office.

Many organizations have a charitable giving department, and while it's important that the people in that department be on board

Deng Lual
Governor's Scholar

COMING BACK HOME

Deng Lual has a dream: Some day, he'd like to work at the United Nations.

He's already developed many of the skills he'll need. For example, he speaks multiple languages fluently and is extremely well spoken in all of them. And he has first-hand knowledge of how the UN operates around the world.

Unfortunately, Deng had to develop those skills in a way that most of us would find unimaginable. Life in Deng's home village of Bor, in Southern Sudan, hadn't changed for thousands of years. But in 1987, a civil war born of a brutal religious and political conflict came to his village. Soldiers from the north burned their homes and killed the residents. Like other small children in his village and in many others, Deng was left with no home, no food, and no family. At the time, he didn't know where his parents were or even if they were still alive.

Deng escaped, walking away from the sound of guns. Hiding from the soldiers, he met up with other children—now known as the "Lost Boys" of Sudan—and walked hundreds of miles, staying alive by eating wild fruit and berries along the way.

Ultimately, he made it to a refugee camp in Ethiopia. When marauders attacked the camp, Deng escaped on foot, again walking hundreds of miles in constant fear of attack and starvation, this time to the Kakuma Refugee Camp in Kenya. Life in the camps was hard, but it kept him relatively safe. Plus, there was a school in Kakuma, which offered him a basic education and some measure of hope.

In time, Deng was given the opportunity to immigrate to the United States through a United Nations resettlement program which granted him refugee status for his protection. Catholic Community Services helped to find him a foster home and a good family even though he was 17, a time when most foster youth are beginning to cope with the reality that they will soon leave the foster-care system.

Today, Deng is a student at Central Washington University as a Governor's Scholar, majoring in Communications. College hasn't always been easy, he admits, it's been a long road to get him there and he is accustomed to dealing with much harder struggles in his young life. With mentoring support in addition to the scholarship, he has been able to get his education on track. Having completed his sophomore year, he is thriving on campus and regularly gives talks and tours to interested groups and prospective students.

One interesting side note: Deng's foster family came to love Deng so much that they moved to Yakima so that they could be close by him to give him support during his college years.

Some day Deng hopes the situation will stabilize at home so that he can return to Sudan. Perhaps he will return to live with his parents who, as it turns out, are living in a Ugandan refugee camp—a bright note in an otherwise tragic situation.

Thanks to the scholarship, not only is Deng's life better but maybe—if his UN dream comes true—the whole world will be a better place as well.

with what you hope to accomplish, it's even more important that you make the opportunity to talk personally with the CEO or head of the organization to hear exactly what his or her major concerns and hopes would be. That conversation might not always happen in the CEO's office—instead, it might take place at a public event or a private party or some other sort of informal get-together. But once you know what's important to the CEO, and once that person has indicated an inclination to support you, then the other key people in the organization are much more likely to give your foundation the focus it needs to put together a successful program.

When talking to CEOs—or to any well-to-do potential benefactors—I often focus on the "investment" angle: Because of our "last-dollar-in" approach to donations, for a reasonably small per-student investment, the organization can have a major impact on education.

Communicate what needs to be done for the children of your state. In Washington, as probably in most states, the state's financial contribution to higher education is going down at the precise time the costs of education are going up, creating a huge gap and ever-bigger barriers for the neediest among us—thus effectively assessing a bigger and bigger burden on our private citizens called "tuition and fees."

> If you think education is expensive, try ignorance. - Derek Bok

This is an opportunity for merchandising! In essence, if you think of it in standard business terms, you are identifying and packaging a whole variety of products that can appeal to a wide variety of people—from individuals of modest means to the wealthiest, from a neighborhood dry-cleaning company to multinational corporations.

You don't need to hard sell most socially conscious benefactors on this point. You do need to communicate to them a simple and clear message. In our case, we focused on the high percentage of children on the free and reduced lunch program that I talked about earlier, which demonstrated the broad need that existed. More than anything, we wanted potential benefactors to realize that more than a third of the young people in the state faced severe financial limitations as they set out to consider the college alternative.

At the same time, we know that many of our benefactors are committed to some very practical business-oriented needs that can benefit from broadening the state's educational base. The needs of education are tightly integrated with the demands of the marketplace. As business in the state grows and thrives, that also increases the need for teachers, nurses, engineers, and scientists. Businesses are better served if people can read better, write better, communicate better, and have improved critical-thinking skills. Ultimately, educated people can get better jobs, pay higher taxes, and become fully engaged in the economy as consumers—once again, we all win! As Jeff Brotman says, "This is in our enlightened self-interest."

In Washington state, we had a notable organization already committed to promoting educational reform—the Gates Foundation. It was important to us to work with them, and we were fortunate that our vision of education aligned closely with theirs.

In other states, there are foundations and individuals of substantial means who may have the same commitment to education—if so, at least part of your work is completed when you walk through the door. At the Washington Education Foundation, for example, we worked closely with Jack Benaroya, a long-time community leader who was looking for opportunities to support young people through a scholarship program. In fact, Jack had already put together something similar to our "Leadership 1000" scholarship all on his own, making a commitment to support several students through their entire college career. He found in us a partner that could help him carry his work forward successfully. That shared purpose we found with Mr. Benaroya is essential to working with every benefactor, but also particularly with individuals or with groups such as departments in corporations.

One of the biggest challenges when putting together scholarship programs with individual benefactors is making sure that they understand that sponsoring a student is a four- to five-year commitment. (Increasingly these days, it's more often five than four.) One-time gifts are great, and you obviously don't want to do anything to discourage them. At the same time, if you're using money from individuals to sponsor a student, you want to be sure that you either have a rock-solid commitment from that individual to support the student through his or her college education, or that you know where the future dollars will come from if the individual is unable or unwilling to continue sponsorship.

You might face the same challenges in working with corporations, but it's less frequently a problem. This wouldn't necessarily be true, however, of a department within a corporation that might come together to sponsor a student or some other groups that you might bring together, such as investment clubs or guilds. Those may be wonderful opportunities, but they offer challenges as well. For example, there may be some doubt that the memberships of those groups will stay together long enough to sponsor students through their entire education. Many departments in most corporations are quite fluid—the people who run and work in the department may change dramatically from one year to the next. Imagining that the department would maintain stability over five years is almost impossible! So while I'd encourage you to pursue getting scholarship support from departments (e.g., setting up donation contests between sales and marketing departments might be one good way to get people motivated and excited about sponsoring students), just be sure that the donation is set up in a way that ensures the student will be supported over the long term. And if you're working with specialized groups, make sure they either have some sort of track record or that you have a back-up plan should something go awry.

Counting on individual donations over time is even less clear cut. A person with good intentions may, for example, face unanticipated financial or medical problems over time that require them to rethink how much money they are prepared to donate. Or their personal motivations may change over time, and they may choose to give to other sorts of causes instead of to education.

Or perhaps an individual might somehow come to be disappointed in the student they have sponsored. At the Washington Education Foundation, we make great efforts to ensure that students and benefactors match up well, and to ensure that students keep in touch on a regular basis if that's what the benefactor wishes. To be honest, we really haven't faced any serious difficulties in this regard. All our students and our benefactors have been terrific. Still, we're quite aware of the possibility that this could happen, and we have contingency plans in place if it ever does.

There is one more category of benefactor that is often the very best one to pursue—other foundations. Many foundations are in a position to make grants, but they're not in a position to tackle the multiple issues involved in managing a full scholarship program. For example, they almost certainly would not have the infrastructure to select the right students, mentor them before and during college, track their performance, support them if they start to falter, and work directly with key contacts in colleges and universities. This would be a tall order—one that's simply business as usual for any foundation focused on education, but not necessarily for other foundations. Many foundations may want to support education but not to the level at which they have to build that entire infrastructure from scratch.

Talking to these other foundations about raising money is, in a sense, simpler and more predictable than the other potential benefactors described here. Typically, they already have a clearly defined purpose. So if your scholarship program matches up with their established objectives, you may be well on the way to getting support. And conversely, if there isn't a match, that's pretty clear right away too, and you can save yourself the time and the energy to pursue other opportunities instead.

What's more, foundations typically have a predictable flow of grant money, so they're in a good position to make the commitment over time than another organization might be. For a foundation that's granting money, putting together a partnership with another foundation such as the Washington Education Foundation to serve as its operational arm can be a real benefit.

But it does require flexibility from the education foundation. In our case, we sometimes work in the background, completely behind the scenes, so that the granting foundation is the only entity recognized. In other situations, such as with the Gates Foundation, we work together as active partners with both foundations contributing significant time and effort. Finally, on other occasions we're at the forefront alone, with the granting foundation wanting simply to make the donation and then feel confident that we'll handle everything from there consistent with their desires.

Ultimately, it's important to keep in mind why you're raising the money in the first place: to help students in need succeed. If you can maintain that focus as you talk with your various potential benefactors, you'll be able to do the best-possible job of representing those students and their financial needs as you go out and talk with various groups and individuals.

John & Ginny Meisenbach

For nearly a decade, John and Ginny Meisenbach have been sponsoring students and helping pay for their college education.

"We're big believers in the importance of education," says John. He and Ginny played a key role in the expansion of Zion Preparatory

Academy—an urban school in Seattle that caters to inner-city kids.

The Meisenbachs partner with the Washington Education Foundation to provide support to high school students who need help financing their college education. As a graduate of White River High School in Buckley, John has focused his efforts on supporting students from his alma mater.

Working with the Foundation's Leadership 1000 scholarship program, John and Ginny set basic parameters for the students they support. The Foundation makes the actual student selections, and then provides whatever level of one-on-one guidance the students need, including appropriate intervention and guidance if they require it. The Foundation provides regular reports to the Meisenbachs, so they don't have to chase down that information by themselves.

At the same time, they're able to have regular contact with the students they support, and serve as the type of role model that these young people so often don't have at home.

"We like the idea of supporting an individual student," John says. "If everybody does a little bit, and enough people start to do it, it can make a huge difference in these students' lives. The consequences could be incredible."

The Stuart Foundation

In the charter document for the Stuart Foundation, founded in the 1930s, E.A. Stuart noted that: "It is my keenest desire that the country's opportunities and its possibilities remain open and available to my son and to my grandchildren and to their children after them as well as to all other men and women who have high ideals and are willing to make sacrifices for their attainment."

"My great grandfather was a God-fearing Quaker who worked until the day he didn't wake up," reminisces Eldridge Stuart. "He put us on the path of caring for our communities."

The Stuart Foundation has supported a wide range of programs in California, including several designed to support the continuing education of foster children. Among the initiatives is the innovative Guardian Scholars program, one aspect of which is that universities are encouraged to keep a dorm open full-time for students who have come out of foster-care situations, since most of them really have no home to go home to. In that sense, the university becomes their home.

"More than 60 percent of kids end up on the streets after they're pushed out of foster care," explains Stuart. "And what's particularly terrible about this is that these kids haven't done anything wrong. It was just the bad luck of the draw that they ended up in a foster-care situation.

"But education can make a huge difference in their lives," he continues. "The less educated not only make less income, but they are also the first to be laid off. By helping them gain more marketable skills, we can support their own personal growth as well as supporting the overall economy."

As an example, Stuart cites a young man who had been bounced around in more than 20 foster-care placements, facing everything from abuse to having his clothes stolen. But he survived; he is graduating this year from Stanford, and is headed for Wall Street.

Recently the Stuart Foundation made the decision to extend its generosity to the state of Washington. First, the Stuart Foundation provides resources which fund our Independent Services activities (we now have close to 400 former foster youth in our scholarship programs). Second, it turned to the Washington Education Foundation to handle the distribution of its contributions here, since the Washington Education Foundation had the existing educational contacts and infrastructure that would allow it to sponsor the kinds of students and programs that they've supported for so long in the state of California.

The value of the contributions, observes Stuart, doesn't stop when the students graduate. "We've seen so many of these young people go back and perform service in their communities, helping other kids who may be facing the kinds of challenges that they did in their lives."

Jeff & Tricia Raikes

Through their sponsorship of three students—two young women at the University of Washington, and one at Eastern Washington University—Jeff and Tricia Raikes have seen the tremendous impact that education can have on these young lives.

"Without support, none of these young people would have been able to attend college," notes Tricia. "But education can go a long way to close the gaps between people in our society, and to level the playing field for everyone to succeed."

"We think of it in terms of ROI—return on investment," Jeff explains. "For the relatively modest investment that's needed to sponsor these students, we're able to see huge returns that pay off not only for them now, but for the rest of their lives. By comparison, without financial support none of them would have been able to attend college at all."

Particularly rewarding to the Raikes has been seeing how their students have blossomed during their college years. "These students are not only getting good grades," notes Tricia, "but they're active in the life of the campus through participation and leadership in various university organizations. What's more, our family has become closely connected to them, not only through the regular reports we receive about their progress, but also through personal connections such as when our children helped put together gift baskets to get our students through their exams.

"There's nothing more energizing than a young mind," Tricia concludes. "Through helping these young people, we're all winners—the students, our family, and society as a whole."

Jack Benaroya

Like other young men of his generation, World War II interrupted Jack Benaroya's dreams of attending college. By the time the war was over he was supporting a family and never was able to go to college.

Mr. Benaroya built a career in real estate development that helped to shape the face of Seattle, and his work drove the growth of the city for generations. He's also one of the city's leading philanthropists, donating to numerous civic causes. Among the most notable was his unsolicited $17 million donation to the Seattle Symphony to build a world-class symphony hall, a donation which helped to spark the enthusiasm and generosity of other benefactors.

But Mr. Benaroya never forgot his roots. A graduate of Garfield High School, he wanted to do something to help graduates of his alma mater attend college—especially African-American men, students who were among the most at-risk group in our population and where he felt he could really make a difference.

At first, he tried to sponsor students all by himself, but quickly he realized that to succeed, these young men needed a full support structure, incorporating advance mentoring to prepare them for college, and they needed follow-up once they got there.

In 2002 he turned to the Washington Education Foundation and offered to sponsor four young men from Garfield at the University of Washington. It has worked. (See the profile of Alex Hatzey, later in this book, who is one of the students sponsored by Mr. Benaroya.) All four men are well on track to graduation. One of them, after meeting with Mr. Benaroya, decided to follow in his footsteps and work toward a career in construction management. The rewards of this program, notes Mr. Benaroya, go well beyond the young men themselves:

"Quality education is the centerpiece of our economy and our society," he observes. "It is our goal to provide motivated people with the opportunity to learn and grow to the very best of their abilities. We are proud to sponsor these worthy and enthusiastic students."

8

WORKING WITH THE GOVERNMENT

WE WOULD HOPE THAT OUR STUDENTS WOULD WANT TO PARTICIPATE in our democracy, and give back to their communities in the same spirit that their communities make education possible for them. We regularly see this result, even as our scholarship recipients perform volunteer work in tutoring, nursing homes, and in high school programs designed to help kids get out of trouble and stay out of trouble.

Occasionally, I'll run into a potential benefactor or legislative representative who will play the devil's advocate with me. They'll say that scholarships are not important; that in fact our state is best served by letting other states pay for the costs of education and then sending their educated kids to us to take the good jobs and big paychecks! My first reaction is to say that's not fair to our kids. But what's more, it's not practical either. The worse the poverty problem in our state, the less attractive our state becomes as a business destination. And if a lot of people in the state are scraping along just trying to make ends meet, it's hardly an ideal environment for business to grow.

All of this, ultimately, points to the importance of public/private partnerships in developing scholarship programs. It isn't enough for private individuals to come forward with monies if those can't be integrated into larger government programs designed to ensure student success.

At the Washington Education Foundation and at our friends and partners at the Gates Foundation, we've concluded that success needs to start not once the student reaches college but before that, in helping students during their middle and high school years to appreciate the potential opportunity of going to college.

The state of Washington sponsors public institutions where these students can attend and, historically, it has kept tuition at a comparatively low cost (although not low enough, regrettably, for the neediest in our society). But with increasing demands on the educational structure and increasing demands from many different groups serving many different needs across the board at the state level, the state has begun to increase tuition costs.

We could sit back and complain about this (and sometimes we do). We could do our best to make the case that these increasing tuition charges are just promoting the gap between rich and poor in our society and costing the state more in the long run than it saves in the short run. (We do our best to make the case for this point as well.)

But more than anything, we know this predicament becomes a call to action for us—a call that allows us to make it crystal clear to benefactors what the needs are close to home. And what's more, it forces us to be extremely crisp and focused on what we need to ask our state to step forward and do.

In Washington, we've determined that we need to advocate for education in a variety of ways and with several different people.

So, for example, while our Achievers Scholarship can support a couple of thousand students every year, we know as we've said before that this support needs to start at the high school level, in the schools itself. As a result, that becomes something that the Superintendent of Public Instruction, who oversees K–12 education, will want to understand and, we hope, support. Our vision has been that since we are providing millions of dollars and thousands of volunteers to work with these high school students through our privately focused activities, the state should support those efforts by doing what they do best—providing the in-school resources to support those children and to assign and oversee the mentors.

HOW WE DID IT AT THE WASHINGTON EDUCATION FOUNDATION

When we first created the Washington Education Foundation, we weren't entirely sure what the shape of it would be. Ann and I were serving together on the HECB, which is Washington state's Higher Education Coordinating Board, a citizens' board made up of nine private citizens and one student. (Recently, Anthony Rose, the student featured later in this book, served in that capacity.)

The HECB's charter is to administer all the state's financial-aid programs for students, as well as to coordinate various aspects of state public policy initiatives. In the early days, we had considered the possibility that the HECB might administer the funds that we'd raise through the Washington Education Foundation. The HECB is an outstanding group, and we knew that it would do a great job of coordination and management.

As we explored the possibility, however, we realized there were a few difficulties with the concept:

- If we raised money and gave it the HECB, the state government would have ultimate control of how this money would be used. And frankly, that might not always be a good thing. So, for example, while we might raise money promising that it would be used with a focus on higher education, the state might determine that it would be better spent supporting other levels of education— or, for that matter, they might use the funds in entirely different ways. So despite the fact the HECB itself might be committed to the same goals that we are, the state as a whole might determine that other commitments took priority. It's a chance we didn't want to take, especially since we were promising potential benefactors that the money would be spent supporting students approaching the university level.

■ The other big concern we had with the HECB managing the funds was that we were talking about some very serious private-sector money—millions of dollars every year; upwards of $200 million dollars over the foreseeable future. Our intention was to augment other efforts that were taking place in the state, not to replace them. However, we recognized that the people writing the budgets in the state would, inevitably, be trying to strike a balance among many different good causes. If suddenly they had a guarantee of tens of millions of dollars, there'd be a real danger that education would fall off the radar of the budget writers, who would view the support of universities as something that was already covered.

So instead of turning these dollars over to the HECB, we decided to set up an independent 501(c)3 foundation, and then asked the HECB for their advice on how we could benefit from the expertise of the many people in that organization that had been working so long on educational initiatives. Both of our organizations shared a common purpose: educating the high-potential low-income students in our state. The HECB provided the expertise, and the Washington Education Foundation provided monies to the students that the HECB was chartered to support.

We've been very fortunate in having the support of Dr. Terry Bergeson, our state Superintendent of Public Instruction, in these efforts. I spoke of champions earlier in the context of private benefactors; Dr. Bergeson has been another champion in helping to carry out the vision of what we're seeking to accomplish.

In thinking about how other states might implement a program similar to what we have accomplished in the state of Washington, it might be useful to explain how the process extends from the Superintendent's office throughout the rest of the legislative process (although it's important to understand that every state will have a slightly different structure and slightly different needs as it implements its individual programs). In the state of Washington, we spend many hours with Dr. Bergeson's staff identifying the specific needs we have, and justifying those needs in a way that allows them to review what we're doing and to determine how our efforts fit into their broader initiatives. There's no doubt her office is quite aware of the needs and completely on board with the importance of finding solutions. Our charter as an organization, therefore, is to demonstrate how our programs fit into their vision of how the transition from high school to college might work.

Once the Superintendent's staff has made a determination of what is appropriate, they include a request to support our program in their budget to the Governor. You'll remember earlier that I talked about the importance of the Governor as a key person in carrying the vision forward. The Governor needs to be convinced there is a real problem, and that our vision of a public–private partnership can go a long way towards solving that problem. If so, the Governor is likely to endorse, with minimal modifications, the recommendations made by the Superintendent's office. If not, we have to realize there are way too many demands on the Governor's time and attentions to assume support.

When the Governor includes our request in the budget, we still have to work very closely with the legislature to ensure that this budget request will be carried all the way through. Inevitably, politics involves the art of compromise. As an organization working to support students in the state of Washington, we don't want to see the potential good we can do compromised away. The message we carry forward each year to the state legislature is, in essence, simply to point out that we have put together $10 million each year in scholarships, and that we've identified more than 1,000 volunteer Hometown Mentors ready to ensure the success of the students who will receive those scholarships. Our request to the state is that they provide us with the financial resources to manage, oversee, and ensure the success of that program, which quite frankly is a great bargain when you think about it—$10 million in scholarships going directly to students, and the state needs to contribute just 10 percent of that amount to support the Hometown Mentor Program. In addition, we are partnering with others to launch the Foster Care to College program.

In Washington, we've been fortunate to have good allies in the legislature, including the Majority Leader in the Senate, the Speaker of the House, the Chair of the Ways and Means Committee and the Chairman of the House Appropriations Committee as well as the Chairs of the Higher Education and Education Committees. We haven't always gotten exactly what we asked for, but at least they have endorsed our intentions and our programs through their funding efforts. More importantly, we seem to have garnered statewide bipartisan support for our work.

Carrying the Story to the Federal Level

Working with representatives in the federal government offers its own set of challenges and opportunities. Unlike the state level, federal officials typically do not get involved with considering individual scholarship programs or grants, but rather provide their support through Pell Grants that go directly to students. But through a variety of grant programs, they might be able to provide seed money that can help you kickstart the foundation for your state. I'd encourage you to think of establishing an early relationship with your delegation in Washington, DC as you begin to shape the

Alex Hatzey
Leadership 1000 Scholar

FIRST GENERATION IN AMERICA, FIRST GENERATION TO COLLEGE

Alex Hatzey's parents arrived in the United States as refugees from war-torn Eritrea shortly before he was born.

It was a long trip from Northeastern Africa to Dallas, where they settled for 10 years. Ultimately, they joined other family members in Seattle in the hope of finding better opportunities for economic advancement.

A graduate of Garfield High School in Seattle, Alex dreamed of attending college, but didn't know how he could afford it. Thanks to the generosity of Jack Benaroya, a noted civic leader in Seattle, Alex and three other students from Garfield were able to pay for their university education.

The grant came as something of a surprise to Alex, who felt he would be hard-pressed to pay for college without scholarship support. An even bigger surprise, however, was when Mr. Benaroya and some of his colleagues took the time to come to the University of Washington campus to meet with him and the other students to talk about their goals and aspirations for the future. A meeting that he thought might take 10 minutes went on for well over an hour with Mr. Benaroya sharing his thoughts and experience with these young scholars.

Alex was impressed. "I know that Mr. Benaroya is an important, successful, and busy person," Alex observes, "but he also seems to be very down-to-earth at the same time. Meeting with him was a great experience for all of us."

Entering his fourth year, Alex is studying investment analysis and property management. He's made the Dean's List and worked as a marketing consulting intern.

Plus, he's gone back to Garfield to mentor other young African-American scholars. "I hope that I can help some kids by being a role model and prove that you can succeed," he says. "Maybe they can reach for their dreams with a little less intimidation by seeing somebody do what they would like to do. I plan to continue giving back to others and am thankful to Mr. Benaroya for giving back to the others and to me—it has had an enormous impact on my education and my life."

framework for your organization, especially your senators and representatives with longevity.

To qualify for a federal grant, you should start by talking directly to the senators that represent your state as well as members of the House of Representatives. Remember, of course, that you don't have to focus simply on the Congressional Representative from the district in which your foundation will be located, because any representative from your state will have a vested interest in helping to improve the continuing education of its students. So don't stop with your local representative. Carry the story on to anybody in Washington who will listen!

It's important that you be prepared to take the time to help these Congressional Representatives understand the concept of what you're trying to accomplish through your foundation. The simple message that you're putting together a public–private partnership and leveraging public money through the private sector—and thus, getting a lot more bang for each buck—can be very effective.

If you already have a financial commitment from business and community leaders in your state, that will go a long way toward getting the time, and more importantly, the attention of your Congressional Representatives. So as the leader of a foundation, it's a bit of a juggling act. To get start-up funds, you not only need to convince your government representatives that you have private support behind you, but you also may need to convince your private benefactors that the government is willing to commit a fair share of funds in order to support education.

Understand, though, that you're not likely to get everything you want from one meeting. Instead, you'll need to establish an ongoing dialog not only with each of your Congressional Representatives but also with their key staff members, who are most likely the ones who will be reviewing your proposals in detail and putting together the actual requests. Once they've endorsed the idea of supporting the start-up efforts of your foundation, they will be the ones who actually request that funds from the Department of Education be allocated for that purpose. While there are never any guarantees, the fact that a request for funds has been made should, in most cases, get you on your way. Still, it's important to remember that your Congressional Representative, like any government official, is balancing a lot of requests, most of them presented with the same commitment and passion that you feel for your foundation. As a result, you need to think of your contact with these representatives in the same way you'd think about selling a long-term program to a potential customer in a business situation—you need to be forthright and have a lot of fortitude, but at the same time you don't want to push so hard that they'll slam the door in your face.

9

STAFFING THE ORGANIZATION

AS YOU SET OUT TO BUILD YOUR ORGANIZATION, it's important to remember that your first hires will likely be the most important.

In fact, other than determining a clear and precise vision for your organization, these hires may be the most important decisions you'll ever make—decisions that will set the tone for what your foundation will become, as well as determine whether you'll get on the path to success or failure.

It's tricky for a number of reasons. For starters, sometimes you'll feel like you just need somebody—almost anybody—to fill chairs and get things going. But those first people you bring on board are likely to hang around (or so you hope!) for a long time. Not only that, for most benefactors, educators and students, they'll be the first point of contact—the face of your foundation.

They'll also have to work hard—very hard—to get your foundation off the ground, tackling everything from setting operational standards and guidelines to figuring out where to buy light bulbs and coffee stirrers.

As a result, these first employees need to be both great team players, ready to do whatever needs to be done, as well as generalists capable of taking on all sorts of random tasks.

At the same time, however, you'll need people who not only deeply share the vision of your foundation, but also possess the sorts of skills that will allow them to make the specialized decisions that demonstrate a deep understanding of the field. Ideally, you'll also want them to have the potential to move into more senior roles later if and when the organization grows.

To do this, you can't just hire the first person that comes along. You have to be ready to wait patiently, taking on a lot of those everyday tasks by yourself. Yet, when those perfect candidates appear, you need to be ready to move quickly to make an offer, so that you don't lose them to another organization.

So it's a fine line to walk, not unlike the challenge faced by any entrepreneurial startup enterprise: Move slowly, but be ready to move quickly!

At the Washington Education Foundation, Ann and I were fortunate to find some highly qualified candidates right from the start—people who were not only highly experienced in education, but also great sports who shared a wonderful camaraderie together, a willingness to work many, many thankless long hours, and who did all this in the midst of a bare-bones office with hardly a desk or chair to be found anywhere. We like to think of it as great fun, because it was! But it represented a lot of hard work as well.

To understand part of what we were initially looking for at the Washington Education Foundation, I want to introduce you to a couple of our original employees. While no other foundation could precisely duplicate the specific skill sets of the people we initially brought on board, reviewing their backgrounds may give you a sense of the kind of people you should try to find.

As noted earlier, once you've identified the initial people to guide the foundation, there's an important thing you need to let them do: their jobs. The universal temptation, of course, is to try and do it all yourself, especially when you're still caught up in the first enthusiasms of creating the organization. And undeniably, you'll want to be actively involved in the initial hiring decisions, as well as to remain completely cognizant of how financial decisions are being made and how money is being distributed.

> The people we initially selected. . .were, in every way, top performers that I would have been proud to work with in any business venture.

At the same time, you hired these people because they're experts, bringing knowledge and skills to the table that you don't necessarily already have yourself. It's important to give them the chance to make key decisions that will drive the organization forward. If the people you hire really share your vision, that's easy to do.

If they don't share your vision, frankly it may be necessary to identify others to take their place. As in any organization, you sometimes may have to face up to internal clashes. To some degree, that's perfectly all right. Remember, this job of distributing scholarships is serious business, and you need to take on the task in the same serious way you would any other important objective. At the same time, don't let those differences get in the way of the foundation's vision. Make sure the discussions are going in positive and productive directions.

I raise this issue because sometimes, in the nonprofit sector, there can be a tendency to be less stringent and demanding than in the private sector. Unfortunately, too many good organizations with laudable goals have ended up by the wayside because they didn't run their operations in a businesslike manner.

The people we initially selected to take the leading roles in the Washington Education Foundation were, in every way, top performers that I would have been proud to work with in any business venture.

For example, let me tell you about our first hire, Steve Thorndill, who is our Executive Director of Education. Steve joined the Foundation after having spent more than twenty years at the University of Puget Sound as the director of Financial Aid and Scholarships (and holding similar posts at Xavier University in

Chicago and at Ohio University). Steve's initial title was Director of Scholarship Programs, which made him responsible for the establishment of our office and programs, for hiring staff and for the overall administration and management of all programs. It was a tall order. But he did a great job implementing it. We were fortunate. Steve sought us out after having made the decision to pursue opportunities to serve the broader scholarship community rather than continuing his single-school focus. Steve had experienced what he characterized as a "pivotal moment" in his life after serving as a Daniel's Foundation consultant in Denver in 1999, where many of the same types of student-access issues we wanted to address here in the state of Washington were being raised. When he came to us, Steve was doing contract work for the upcoming legislative session on a subject he had chosen for his master's thesis in 1971 at Ohio University—and which we also recognized was central to the entire consideration of scholarship programs:

> Which model is better for an educational system—high tuition accompanied by a high degree of financial aid or low tuition with lower levels of financial aid?

In exploring this and other scholarship-related issues, Steve had attended a presentation in the fall of 2000 by Dr. Deborah Wilds in which she introduced some of the initial program plans from the Gates Foundation to redesign schools and offer scholarships to low-income, underserved students. Steve recalls that he was extremely excited on both a professional and a personal level. Professionally, he saw this as a chance to provide scholarships and other opportunities to many kids being left behind by the system. On a personal level, he saw it as a way that he could contribute that would be consistent with the new direction he wanted to pursue—to be able to manage some part of such a program.

He was directed to us, and we all clicked right away. Ann met with him first, showing him the job description and getting his feedback on what he could do for us. Dr. Deborah Wilds met with him a few days later to ensure that there would be a match and that they could effectively work together. By the time I met with him in the Costco cafeteria shortly after that, my main question was very simple and direct: "You think you can do this job?"

We hired him immediately when we saw that he could hit the ground running. Within a few weeks he had completed his contract work for the legislative session and he was on board.

Shortly after Steve joined us, we hired Tanguy Martin, who now serves as our Executive Director of Finance and Administration. Tanguy Martin initially signed on as our Manager of Systems and Technology, in which he was responsible not only for designing and managing the technological infrastructure of the Foundation itself, but also for facilitating the integration of systems and technology with our high school, college, and business partners. Tanguy came to us with ten years of experience at Seattle University in systems and computer technology, which included work as a Program Analyst and as Project Manager for a broad range of activities, which included serving as Director of Enrollment Services Technology. Tanguy is not only the kind of guy who's extremely self-sufficient and enjoys running his own show (both essential characteristics for any IT manager in any sort of organization), but he also has a great ability to think about systems not only in terms of whether they get the job done today, but also whether they'll continue to work well into the future.

Thanks to Tanguy, we were able to make a lot of smart decisions right from the start—such as decisions about management and tracking systems—that we're still using and benefiting from today. What's more, he's the kind of person who's not afraid to roll up his shirt-sleeves and get his hands dirty—which means we didn't have to call in expensive outside help every time we needed a bit of technology tweaked or repaired.

Once Steve and Tanguy and a few other critical first people were in place, and once the first scholarship programs went into development, Ann and I depended on them to make the day-to-day decisions that evolved from our initial vision. They were both up to the task of helping to drive that vision farther. The Foundation grew thanks in great part to their outstanding management and leadership. They were able not only to tackle the "do-it-all" role that was required when we were getting started, but also to take on increasing management responsibilities as our staff grew. In short— we couldn't have done it without them!

"PEAC" PERFORMANCE

As you read about each of these initial staff members of the Foundation, and think about the kinds of people you might want to consider for your initial hires, you'll notice certain common characteristics, all summed up by a formula that we might shorthand as "PEAC." We decided to identify people who can bring peak performance to an organization according to the following criteria:

PASSION—A deep-seeded belief that higher education can make a difference, along with the drive and desire to bring children of need into the educational system.

EXPERIENCE—While experience doesn't necessarily have to come from within the educational arena, think in terms of finding people who can complement your own experience. If you're an educational expert, it may be worthwhile to see what the business community has to offer. If you rose up through the entrepreneurial ranks of a corporation, finding educational specialists will help give you perspective that could be very difficult to develop all by yourself.

APTITUDE—It almost goes without saying that you need to hire smart, accomplished people. But it's important not to lose sight of

117

the fact that it's not enough just to have passion—your employees need to have the skills and the know-how to get the job done.

COMMITMENT—As one of our first staff members noted, on the day he arrived at the Foundation there was "no furniture, no computers, nothing but a lot of work that needed to get done, and done quickly." If your employees aren't ready to give 150 percent right from the start, you'll never get off the ground. If they are, your foundation can soar.

Sample Start-Up Foundation Organizaton Chart

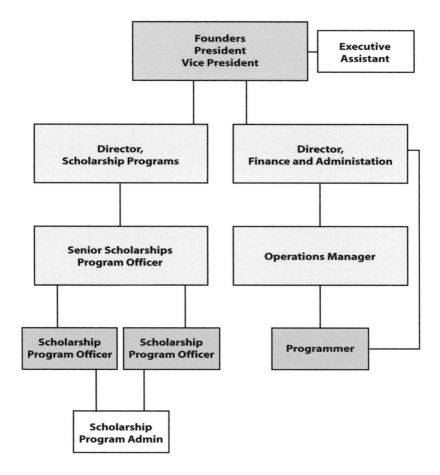

10

MENTORING

MORE THAN ANYTHING ELSE, THE APPROACH of the Washington Education Foundation is distinguished from other programs by our use of mentors.

Our Hometown and College Mentoring programs were originally conceived as vital components of the Achievers Scholarship Program. Targeting underrepresented populations for college scholarships presents unique challenges. Students from these populations typically don't have any family or cultural experience that would provide familiarity with the requirements for applying to and succeeding in higher educational institutions. The mentor programs were designed to offer that much-needed support system.

The mentor's role in the student's life is unique. The mentor is not a parent, a babysitter, a social worker, a nurse or a judge. Instead, the mentor serves as a trusted guide, a role model who can help the student develop the awareness of the choices in his or her life. The mentor helps students prepare for college by ensuring they take the proper preparatory classes, select an appropriate college for their interests, and handle their application forms and scholarship paperwork properly.

Mentors are often described as coaches, guides, confidantes, cheerleaders, role models, and advocates. In truth, mentors are all of these and much more. It's a huge responsibility because mentors can have a huge impact—one student at a time.

It's important to remember that the hundreds of mentors who have signed up for our program are all *volunteers*, committed individuals who want to have a direct impact on the self-esteem and healthy growth of a young person. We're proud of what our scholarship programs have achieved. I can say for certain that without the volunteer support of our wonderful mentors, we literally couldn't have done it without them.

How Hometown Mentors Are Selected and Matched to Students

Currently, we have more than 575 high school students supported by approximately 400 Hometown Mentors—yes, some of them enjoy the opportunity so much that they commit to working with more than one student.

In spring, these mentors take on double duty, supporting not only their graduating students, but an additional new crop of incoming scholarship recipients.

Mentors are selected from people in the community who value higher education and share with the Foundation the goal of helping young people obtain a four-year college degree.

Mentors come from all walks of life—from school-district superintendents and school principals to accountants and retirees—a total cross-section of the population. Mentors are kind, concerned adults—young and old, from all walks of life—who want to offer youth support, guidance, and encouragement. But they are *not* expected to be foster parents or to solve *all* of the problems of youth. Instead, the mentor is meant to be focused on the everyday challenges of school, society, and community by drawing upon their own greater knowledge and experience. By connecting with students, the mentors offer a way to expand their horizons and to increase the likelihood of future success.

The mentor is an adult guide—a person who can open the pathway to college for students. Many of them have been down the same path in their lives as our students, others may have enjoyed an easier path to college and want to ensure that students today can have the best-possible chance to reach college and have the best chance of success when they get there.

Each of the schools in which we provide scholarships has on staff a College Preparatory Advisor—what we call a CPA—to oversee the student and mentoring programs. The CPAs consider a wide variety of factors—including mentor availability, location and, most especially, skills and interests—in order to determine a customized best possible one-to-one match for each student. Because the CPAs develop a deep appreciation of both student needs and mentor capabilities, they're able to create situations in which students can thrive and mentors can do the most-possible good.

How Hometown Mentors Work with High School Students

At least once each month (more often, when possible) mentors sit down with students to talk about academic and career goals, progress on college planning, and the financial aid process. To many students, most of this is a mystery. Some of the students we support have never really thought much about their future careers. To be honest, the future has always been a somewhat scary concept to many of them. Even those who have thought about their future have never fully understood the link between what they're learning in school and what they'll ultimately do in life.

College planning is even more mysterious. When do you have to sign up for the SAT? How do you make sense of your SAT scores? Is it OK to take the test a second time—and is it ever a bad idea? How many colleges should you apply to? What sorts of schools are worth the application effort, and which ones are not good fits for the student? Do you have to declare a major before you apply? How

Estakio Beltran
Achievers Scholar

FINDING A HOME

Like other foster children, Estakio Beltran lived a turbulent young life. He escaped an abusive father to enter the foster-care system, but ended up being transferred from one home to another. He attended nine different high schools before finally finding a stable home in his senior year.

At times, he had to ride the bus for four hours each day just to remain in the same school. He discovered he had a talent and a passion for gymnastics. He he was good enough, in fact, to participate in the U.S. Olympic Committee's FLAME (Finding Leaders Among Minorities Everywhere) program in Colorado Springs, where he met several Olympians. But finding a foster home near a gym where he could train and teach wasn't always possible, even though it was the one activity he enjoyed most.

"Vaulting was my passion," he says, "probably because it was so symbolic. I wanted to travel a straight path, but there was always an obstacle in my way, and I had to figure out how to get over it." It was a long, hard road for a very young man to travel.

Estakio had a goal: to be the first foster child ever in Eastern Washington to attend a four-year university while still a ward of the state. It had never happened before. There were no real guidelines on how to proceed.

The biggest obstacle was the economic one: As a foster child, he had no source of financial support beyond public assistance, which wouldn't be enough to get him into a four-year program.

Through the support of Ann Ramsay-Jenkins and the Washington Education Foundation, he was able to receive a scholarship and obtain admission to Gonzaga University.

It's been full speed ahead for Estakio ever since. He's served as a youth representative to the Washington State Legislature and as chief legislative officer for the Gonzaga University Student Advisory Committee where he advises on foster-care and minority-student issues. As an ambassador for foster youth and orphans, he has traveled extensively throughout Europe, Latin America, and Africa. In August 2003, he was awarded the prestigious Golden Tennis Shoe Award, given annually by Washington Senator Patty Murray for outstanding citizenship. He is now working on children's issues in the office of Senator Maria Cantwell. What's more, he's even become a published poet.

Today, Estakio speaks regularly at conferences and meetings, inspiring young people to make the most of the talents and the intelligence they've been given. Obviously, Estakio has plenty of both!

long does it take to fill out an application? What should you say in the application essay? What shouldn't you say? Should you apply for early admission or not? How much time does it take to hear back from the college? If you're accepted to more than one school, how do you decide which one is best for you? And then there's financial aid. What are the rules, restrictions, requirements, and opportunities available to students in need?

Frankly, most of those questions slow and stymie even students from middle- and upper-income households with a strong family college tradition. So can you imagine how much more difficult it is for a low-income student to make sense of it all, when typically he or she is the first person in the family, and maybe the only person among their acquaintances, to plan for college.

That's where the Hometown Mentors come in, offering the students a roadmap to the college experience, and helping them get back on track if and when they ever lose their way in the process. The mentor provides the student with somebody to turn to for everything from everyday college concerns to major life decisions. More than anything, mentors share the knowledge and the skills necessary so that the students can make the system work for them. Mentors offer perspective on how students can best focus their efforts. In this way students, will know which small concerns are, indeed, small and which issues require immediate and serious attention.

A couple of key footnotes to establishing a mentor program, which may seem obvious in many ways but which should definitely not be forgotten:

- The student's parent or guardian needs to give written permission for the student to participate and to have a direct route for communication with the person overseeing the mentor should any problems or concerns occur. At the Washington Education Foundation, we also send out periodic correspondence to ensure that all lines of communication are staying open.

- The students need to agree to participate in the program, and to sign a contract committing themselves, among other things, to adhere to our Washington State Achievers Scholars Expectations and to meet, at minimum, once a month with the mentor.

- The meetings between student and mentor always take place on the school campus in a public location such as the library, cafeteria, etc.

- The school's administration and counseling staff needs to receive regular communications from the scholarship organization so that they can best support the students, ensuring that the mentors' efforts augment the school's existing activities.

- The mentors have to maintain a regular log of their meetings with students in order to document that meetings have occurred, describe the topics discussed, and note the progress made toward completing the students' tasks. Mentors are also instructed to take any special problems or concerns to the College Preparatory Advisors.

How Does the College Mentoring Program Operate?

Like the Hometown Mentors, the College Mentors are volunteers who give of their time and energy to help students succeed. Quite often, they are people associated with the university in some capacity, such as a professor or staff member. The College Mentoring program varies widely from one school to the next because the students entering those colleges have such different needs and cultures.

For example, a student at the University of Washington—a very large campus—faces different challenges than a student attending a smaller college. At the University of Washington, the student may have a greater challenge just dealing with the shock of walking on to a campus that could literally be larger than his or her hometown. And the fact that the students may not know anyone in any of their classes, and not recognize any of the same students from class to class, can be challenging for any student new to the college experience. At the same time, the size of the University of Washington means that it can offer a host of opportunities and classes that a smaller campus can't.

We celebrate these differences but at the same time, we recognize that it makes more sense to work closely with the universities to create a program appropriate to their environments around a basic skeleton of how a program might operate. One thing that is universally important is that the mentors must be assigned to the students from the moment they hit the campus and that they need to be there right from the earliest days to help them navigate through the confusions of campus life. Remember again that many of these students are first-generation college students whose parents are often not able to share the first-hand experience about what is important. Something students often have to learn, for example, is to move beyond the classic K–12 mentality that typically doesn't invite the student to challenge the teacher. At the university, in seminars and other situations, professors are not only open to intellectual challenges from their students, but they expect it.

11

Building the Infrastructure

WE WERE EXTREMELY FORTUNATE, RIGHT FROM THE START of the Washington Education Foundation, to enjoy the enthusiastic support of Jim Sinegal, Jeff Brotman, Dick DiCerchio, and all of the Costco team. In addition to donating money, energy, time, they gave us something that we quickly discovered was invaluable: an infrastructure.

As a highly successful company, Costco had a well-established infrastructure that a start-up organization could only envy. They had space. Phone systems. Computers. Servers. Net connections. Photocopy machines. And an outstanding staff of people to set up and support all that equipment. To an established company, it all may seem rather mundane—the everyday stuff of running a business. But for a foundation such as ours, it was literally a godsend. Especially because, in some ways, we weren't particularly patient! We wanted to fast-start our program and get as many students on to the university path as quickly as we could. Without the support of our corporate champion, Costco, it would have probably taken us a year or two to reinvent the wheel and build these systems all by ourselves. With the support of Costco, we were up and running in just weeks, not years. Costco was able to leverage its existing infrastructure by allowing us to piggyback on their reasonably mature systems. So, for example, when they installed computer servers for the travel department in our building, they were able also to help us with our installations at the same time. And when we had any difficulties with our phone system, they could make the call for us—let's be honest, a big company like Costco has clout that a start-up foundation doesn't!

So Tanguy Martin could spend his time overseeing the installation of these office systems rather than creating it all from scratch. And what's more, he could focus his energies on exploring and putting together accounting systems, a benefactor tracking system, and a scholarship management system.

As I say, Costco's involvement made a huge difference to us. At the same time, there are a few things that start-up foundations should keep in mind when working with any corporate sponsor:

- Some of the decisions you might make in a start-up operation can be quite different from what you'd do in an established organization.

- Similarly, some of the business objectives of a company may not track precisely with the objectives of your foundation. A business, for example, typically has to concern itself with inventory issues. The biggest inventory issue for your foundation may be how many pencils to keep on hand for student programs. So the systems that work for them may not always transfer easily and automatically to your organization.

- Finally, it's important to remember that after the initial set-up stage the sponsoring company may need to reduce its commitment, either because it's moving on to other projects or because the growth of your foundation has created challenges well beyond their original commitment. Plus, as your foundation grows, you will want to customize how you do things which, as noted earlier, may prove to be different from your sponsor's approaches. This obviously would have staffing as well as technology implications.

From the beginning, then, it's useful to think about a timeframe in which your organization will take over—and it's important to start being aware of those transitional issues in plenty of time. One place where this issue might arise, for example, is in terms of your website. While the sponsoring organization may help to set it up and host the site on its servers, you may eventually want to host it yourself, on your own servers, to give you maximum flexibility in how it evolves and in how it is updated. Planning the switchover early will make the transition go much more smoothly.

In the same spirit that Costco supported the Washington Education Foundation in our formative stages, we are supporting the Washington State Mentoring Partnership, which was re-launched in 2004 to provide mentors to many young people in our state to help them navigate the obstacles they confront in their lives. An independent organization, the Mentoring Partnership can still enjoy the advantages of our infrastructure, from using our existing phone lines to sharing our website.

At the same time, eventually we would assume that the Mentoring Partnership would grow to a stage at which it will need its own independent infrastructure. Right now, they have four staff members—pretty much the same as we did when we got started in 2000. As it grows, we expect to pass along many of these system-oriented responsibilities to them.

SOFTWARE DECISIONS

In addition to the basic word processing and email software that is required in any office any more, there were three basic types of tools that we needed to implement to manage our scholarship efforts. Two of them we found available commercially; the third we had to build ourselves:

1. **Accounting software.** The temptation at first might have been to select one of the popular small business software tools, such as QuickBooks, since much of the job of accounting for a foundation isn't that different from what would be required to manage any small organization.

   But there are some critical differences. The requirements of non-profit accounting are not entirely the same as what a for-profit business would have to report to the IRS. As a result, we identified an accounting software tool designed not only for non-profits, but also one that could intelligently handle multiple funding sources and give us the ability to account for each individual block of money, such as allocating indirect costs to them if appropriate.

2. **Benefactor tracking system.** Fortunately, there's also good commercial software available for tracking contributions and pledges. As you can imagine, there are plenty of issues to be considered here—from how to recognize and follow up on multi-year pledges to the question of how to follow an individual benefactor's contribution all the way to its intended purpose, either to support an institution or an individual student.

   A good benefactor tracking system is critical because it's a fundamental part of establishing a quality relationship with the people who contribute to your organization. You don't want to forget about pledges made in the past; you don't want to risk alienating good benefactors by making inaccurate reports of their donation (such as in your annual report) or by asking too many times for a contribution. A good system will help you track and stay on top of this important information.

3. **Scholarship tracking system.** The third system—the one that actually follows the students—we had to build ourselves. And we felt that was appropriate. Scholarships are our core business, and we think we understand as well as anybody the requirements for developing a good scholarship tracking system. What we came up with was a program we called SMART (Scholarship and Mentoring Administration and Reporting Tool). SMART is designed to track the entire scholarship process—all the way from the application to ongoing scholarship grants and every step of the way through a student's entire college experience.

   a. SMART supports the actual selection process. Data from the applications we receive are entered into SMART, and we use it to keep track of the information we examine on each of the individual students. This is particularly important for scholarship programs such as ours because we typically include non-traditional and non-cognitive factors when we select a student. It isn't as simple as just plugging in the student's grade point average. Instead, we need to track a number of factors that will help us determine if each student is likely to be successful in college.

   b. We also use SMART to track address and other basic information about students on an ongoing basis. This may seem fairly mundane, but when you consider that we're giving out thousands of scholarships every year, it's not unusual for at least several hundred of those students to move, change phone numbers, change email addresses, etc. By keeping this information updated on a regular basis, we're able to be in close contact with our student population whenever necessary. It's also worth noting that some low-income students may come from migrant families or from family situations in which they need to change households relatively frequently. We don't want to take any chance that those students could lose their scholarships due to turmoil and other challenges that may exist at home.

c. SMART not only keeps track of the dollars that we give to students in scholarships, but it also is critical to our efforts to provide the "last dollar in" when we make a donation. So, for example, if it costs $15,000 to attend a particular university, one student might have received other grants worth $12,000; while the second student received other grants worth $9,000. Our goal is to complement those other grants for which the students qualify. So the first student would receive a grant of $3,000, and the second student would receive a grant of $6,000. In each case, our goal is to be the last dollar in so that the students have the money they actually need to attend the university.

d. All this requires us to have good systems for exchanging data with the institutions where our students attend—another task of the SMART program. We can make sure that all the information in this complex equation is being accounted for with this system.

As you can imagine, however, this is a highly flexible process, which needs to be reevaluated on a regular basis. A student might lose a particular grant one year, and need more money the next year to make up the difference. A student might be given a grant later in the process, or receive additional funds through a secondary source, and not need as much, allowing us to take that money and give it to other students in need.

What's more, the costs of tuition and the costs of living keep going up. So what a student needed in his or her freshman year may be dramatically different from what's needed as a senior.

To be honest, it would be simpler in terms of software and administration just to give a standard grant amount to all students. But it wouldn't work nearly as well. Say you gave every student $5,000. For starters, that money would go a lot farther for the students attending public institutions than for the ones going to private universities. A lot of the students don't need that much, thanks to other scholarship support. Some students need more, and the $5,000 does no more than tease them with the possibility of college without actually having enough money to attend.

That's why we've made the decision to focus on this aid gap, because we think that's how we can really make a difference. We've been through a few generations of SMART and we are close to completing our web-based version in early 2006. When that happens, we'll be able to offer that as a tool to other foundations that face the same sorts of challenges we've already learned how to tackle.

12

DEFINING AND MEASURING SUCCESS

THE MAIN GOAL OF THE WASHINGTON EDUCATION FOUNDATION is simple:

Every student awarded a scholarship will earn a baccalaureate degree.

So everything we do at the Foundation is geared toward high retention. We've been gratified at the kinds of results we've seen from the students we've supported. For example, as noted earlier, more than 60 percent of the students who have been recipients of our first Achievers Scholarships will complete their degrees. This compares to the fact that typically only 25 percent of students in this low-income population manage to complete their degrees. And let's not forget that an awful lot of other qualified students never even get the opportunity to try college at all.

That 60 percent is a good number, well in line with the initial goals we set for ourselves. But we want to do better. The only way we can improve, and know that we've been successful, is to have systems in place right from the start to track our students through their college experiences.

In this chapter, we want to talk about the importance of collecting and managing that data, and then using it proactively to modify scholarship programs. Goals and objectives are a good thing—they help to keep organizations focused, and they help you to understand where you should dedicate your resources and your energies. Even when a company falls short of its objectives, the information is valuable in that it helps you determine whether you may not have had adequate resources in place to meet those objectives, or whether your objectives were even the right ones in the first place. In either case, by tracking the information carefully, you can steer the company onto the right track.

It's the same with granting scholarships to students. Admittedly, it takes time and resources to stay on top of all that data, especially with thousands of students dispersed across dozens of schools. Different students follow different paths to their degrees—some are on a straight-line, fast-track four-year path; some take sabbaticals or other sorts of breaks to travel or experience the world; some simply can't complete all the classes they need for graduation in a four-year period—an increasing challenge for many students. Still, by keeping track of this information, we not only are able to ensure that our scholarship dollars are being properly allocated, but we can also sit back and perform a detailed program review on a regular basis and look for ways to fine-tune what we're doing. Sometimes the solution involves a few pinpointed interventions with highly qualified individual students who are struggling for reasons unrelated to their own intelligence and personal drive. Because of our active mentoring program, we were able to assist Olatokunbo Olaniyan— the young woman featured earlier in this book—at a critical point in her college career.

But often, we need to evaluate how the programs themselves are working, to ensure that we'll be able to successfully identify the next Olatokunbos when they face particular sorts of challenges. And what's more, we need to be sure that we've identified the *right* students to attend college. As noted earlier, many of the measures we use in the selection of students are non-traditional. Our 60 percent success rate suggests that these selection processes are working, but we wouldn't know that if we didn't carefully track the data. Not only that, it's essential that we're able to share our success record with our benefactors, particularly those organizations and individuals that want to play an active role in the education of the students they support. These can be groups, such as the Gates Foundation, that want to ensure that their contributions are leading to good results. But we've also noted that many individual benefactors, such as those who sponsor students through the Leadership 1000 scholarship, want to have a personal and direct understanding of how their dollars are working.

Remember: most of those individuals came from the business world as well, and they're accustomed to seeing the same sorts of projections that I did. One good aspect of our benefactor tracking system is that we are able to link donations with the students they support, so we're in a good position to provide that information to anyone who wants it.

13

ARIZONA COLLEGE SCHOLARSHIP

FOUNDATION CASE STUDY

There are some interesting parallels between Governor Christine Gregoire of Washington State and Governor Janet Napolitano in the state of Arizona that precede their rise to the governorships of their respective states. Both were former Attorneys General, a role in which they got to know each other well. Both are cancer survivors. And both of them have a deep-seated commitment to promoting economic growth through the support of education.

Early in her term, I had the opportunity to attend a breakfast sponsored by Governor Gregoire and sat next to Governor Napolitano, who was exploring how best to meet the needs of education in her state. Many of the needs are the same. For example, approximately 45 percent of K–12 students in Arizona are eligible for free and reduced-price lunches, as in Washington state, suggesting a huge financial need. By their estimate, each year more than 5,000 low-income high-potential high school graduates in Arizona don't attend college because they can't afford it. And they figure that's a conservative estimate. Tuition was on the rise—more than 30 percent in just two years—due to budget cuts and reduced state aid at Arizona universities.

But there are some notable differences as well, not only in the cultural mix of the low-income students (with greater percentages of Latina/Latino and Native American students), but also in the fact that the state does not have as many universities and, perhaps most critically, does not offer student aid at the state level.

Because of our experience with the Washington Education Foundation, the state of Arizona asked for our help. As Dr. Paul Koehler, Education Advisor to Governor Napolitano, recalls, there were several aspects of our program that they looked to as a model for what they wanted to do:

1. Funding scholarships through private donations from individuals, corporations and other foundations
2. Being able to be flexible about the types of programs that could be developed based on what benefactors want to do, while still working from a strong consistent mission
3. Establishing an efficient organization for distributing scholarship dollars
4. And the fact that we were tracking students such that we could identify our successes and intelligently evaluate ways to do better

We worked closely with Paul and the Governor to get them started, mirroring many of the same things that we did in the state of Washington. For example, the Governor brought together approximately 25 leaders from across the state to sit down together and explore what needed to happen. These leaders came from all walks of life—business and community leaders, elected officials and policymakers, philanthropists and foundations, education leaders, and community service leaders—a real cross-section of the state.

Being quite busy in her first term, the Governor was scheduled to spend only about 15 minutes in our first session. She stayed for more than an hour.

By the end of the second meeting, Don Budinger of the Rodel Foundation—which has a long record of supporting education— asked who among those state leaders would be willing to stay together and serve as a steering committee for the new Arizona College Scholarship Foundation. Every hand in the room went up. Many of these same individuals donated start-up money along with Costco and the National Education Foundation—and this Arizona effort was launched in March 2005. Martha Harmon was selected as CEO and Executive Director. Already, she's initiated a pilot scholarship program and started putting all the organizational pieces in place to identify qualifying students.

Some of the programs they establish will be, we all believe, similar to what we've done in Washington State. Some approaches will be different. For example, Martha says that they may need to start mentoring at a much younger age since so many young people drop out of school so early.

"Our steering committee members have been quite generous," she observes, "and Arizona is a state in which people are accustomed to working collaboratively. I'm confident some of the programs they establish will, we all believe, be quite successful."

Don, who has been generous in shepherding the Rodel Foundation's support of the Arizona College Scholarship Foundation, noted: "We have been honored to be the first foundation replicating the wonderful work done by the Washington Education Foundation. Thanks to the inspiring model from Washington, Arizona is now fully committed to putting together an equally successful scholarship opportunity for our high-potential low-income high school students."

Anthony Rose
Achievers Scholar

FROM HISTORY TO THE FUTURE

Even in high school, Anthony Rose had a great appreciation for history. A big challenge for him, he recalled, was coming to grips with the realization that some of his early historical heroes had, in fact, performed excessive injustices. He had to unlearn the facts that had been burned into his mind like a branding iron since kindergarten.

It wasn't the only struggle he had had to face in his young life. Raised in a single-parent household, the oldest of five children, money was always an issue in his family. Anthony started working and paying for everything himself, so that the money his mom brought in could be spent on the other kids.

Working a job didn't help his grades. His counselors, perhaps not recognizing his potential, recommended he enter the military rather than following his dream to go to college.

Fortunately for Anthony, he had a mom who pushed him to pursue his dreams, whatever it took. "If you want something, you go for it!" she told him.

Anthony had always challenged himself in school, taking advanced courses even when other people thought he was pushing himself too hard. One of his favorite classes was Speech and Debate. He's a natural on stage, the kind of speaker who inspires everyone in the room to step up and take action. People at his high school still talk about a memorable speech he gave at a Martin Luther King assembly. That speech was just the start of his civic awareness activities.

In September 2001, as a recipient of an Achievers Scholarship and preparing for his freshman year at the University of Washington, Anthony was attending the University of Washington's Office of Minority Affairs Summer Bridge Program. The Program is designed to help students like him make the transition into college. After the terrible events of September 11th, he found himself remembering history and that the conventional wisdom about events wasn't necessarily the truth.

Observing what he felt were terrible anti-Arab activities, he and others in the program joined together in a quiet protest against what they felt was a new emergence of racism. "Before we accuse people of doing something wrong," he said at the time, "we should work to understand what's happening." One thing led to another, and the next thing he knew he was participating in an MSNBC panel on television, representing a student point of view. It was, as he said, the emergence of his political side—one that fit naturally with his love of history, but which hadn't really come to the forefront before.

Since then, Anthony has been recognized for his great skills and his excellent leadership potential. Recently, he was selected to join 250 students and young community leaders from across the country at the first Next Generation Democratic Youth Leadership Summit in Washington, DC. He has served as President of the Black Student Commission, President of the Black Student Union, and President and Director of Community Outreach for the Phi Beta Sigma Fraternity. Anthony was recently nominated as the International Collegiate of the Year for 2005 and became the International Oratorical Champion for 2005. And to top it all off, Anthony was the student representative on the state of Washington's Higher Education Coordinating Board.

None of it would have been possible if Anthony hadn't gone to college. And college might not have happened for him without the scholarship support of the Washington Education Foundation. And none of it would have happened without his mother, who taught Anthony the most important lesson of all: to believe in himself.

14

Going Forward
Flexibility for the Future

FLEXIBILITY IS AN ESSENTIAL STRENGTH of the Washington Education Foundation. Ours is not a cookie-cutter approach to scholarships, but rather we have evolved to fit changing parameters of benefactors at the same time we continue to meet the needs of students. Like any vibrant organization, we're reinventing ourselves each and every day. While the needs haven't changed dramatically, more and more opportunities continue to reveal themselves. For example, we started our Foundation with the broad charter of supporting high-potential low-income students. Over time, we've increasingly brought sharper focus to these efforts as we worked with great organizations like Costco, the Gates Foundation, Château Ste. Michelle, and others, and built programs that complemented their generous efforts. We've pinpointed particular needs—such as the needs of foster children and the increasing need for support of educational efforts in the sciences—and sought out experts to help us craft programs to better meet those needs, as well as benefactors who could bring their enthusiastic support to them. We've looked for opportunities to support even more students by proactively developing innovative programs such as Leadership 1000 in which we look to match up specific students with specific benefactors in a way that creates even more wonderful student success stories. And, we've expanded our vision beyond the needs in Washington state alone, and begun working toward supporting the growth and development of other foundations in other states through the creation of the National Education Foundation.

The result is that while the overriding vision and our larger goals remains the same, the specific ways we seek to accomplish those goals may change over time. When we started the Washington Education Foundation, it was enough just to be offering scholarships to some number of students that otherwise would be left behind. Now, we're constantly looking for ways to expand the number of students we can support, and to ensure that these students are successful in receiving their college degrees.

It's a tall order, and we've been incredibly gratified by the level of support we've received from our benefactors—both those who have given of their money and time—as well as by the ever-improving level of performance by our students as we fine-tune our programs.

There are many common elements that we've come to believe are ultimately essential in any programs we develop, including the following:

- **Identifying potential recipients early in the process.** Wait too long, and you've lost them! Identify them early, and the Foundation can help guide these high-potential students toward what will ultimately be a highly successful college experience.
- **Providing mentoring and support from the start.** Since these kids often don't have educational backgrounds in their home settings, mentoring is essential. Sometimes that mentoring takes place in a formalized way, such as the Hometown Mentor program we've implemented in the Achievers Scholarship Program. And sometimes they're less formal relationships—something as basic

as our staff members making sure that students are properly following the application process, and helping to get them on track if they haven't been.

■ **Focusing on four-year colleges, not trade schools or community colleges.** We want to support all types of education, and we recognize the incredible importance of ensuring that there is a full spectrum of educational opportunities available to students. At the same time, as a single organization, we have only so much time and so many resources we can focus on educational needs. Our charter has been, and will continue to be, focused on helping students receive baccalaureate degrees because we believe that is an area in which many low-income students *can* succeed, if only given the chance. We will leave it to other great organizations and government agencies to think about exactly where these other educational alternatives should fit into the mix.

■ **Remaining student centered.** It's all about the young people, and all about how we can dedicate our time and our energies to best support their education.

The above elements are where we stand firm. As we discussed in Chapter 3, in order to succeed, any organization has to be sharply focused on where it's going and what it wants to accomplish. But as suggested above, it's important to remember that to be successful an organization also has to be flexible at times in order to take advantage of changing opportunities, evolving needs, and what in the business world we would call "market conditions." Some of the changeable elements can include:

■ **Types of fundraising programs.** What worked in the past may not necessarily work in the future. Even with highly successful programs, such as the Costco breakfast, we discuss every year what we can do better and differently in order to ensure that the program continues to grow—and grow intelligently. For example, we hold the Costco breakfast at one of the two recipient universities. If we wanted to, we could find more space for more people in other facilities. Right now we believe it's important, however, for the benefactors to literally step foot on campus, so they get a first-hand experience of what these colleges are like and so they can sit with potential student recipients at each table. We'll sacrifice the opportunity to add more tables to the event for what we believe is the greater benefit gained from offering this direct view of where the programs are being implemented.

Still, we remain open to any organization that is looking to support the needs of students. We want to try to work with them in an innovative and flexible way that's consistent with their own culture and operations. So, for example, Château Ste. Michelle—which sponsors a wonderful series of public concerts every summer that are extremely popular—added one more concert to support scholarships. It's a great program, consistent with what they already do, supported through a well-established concert infrastructure (it's no small task to put on one of these), and the proceeds make a huge difference in the lives of many students.

■ **Visibility of the Foundation.** Sometimes as a foundation we are publicized up front; sometimes we are working in the background. This basically goes back to the point made above, about being student-centered. Our goal ultimately is to support the students, not to get a lot of press for ourselves. To do that, we'll flexibly fit in wherever and however the sponsoring organization wants—from taking a relatively minor role to running the whole show. Sometimes this evolves over time, on different programs. A sponsoring organization might want a major role in the first years of a program, but it may want to effectively put things on autopilot after that. The opposite can also be true—the sponsoring organization might ask us to take over all the details in the beginning (since we've done it all before), but to learn from our experience and increase their role over time. Once again, it doesn't matter to us. We remain flexible so that the students can ultimately benefit.

- **Working with individuals, firms, corporations, and gifting foundations.** Our initial benefactor base was built from generous corporate and foundational grants. Over time, we've significantly increased the amount of money raised from individuals and private firms. While we continue to work with all these different types of organizations, we see tremendous opportunities going forward with the generous gifts of a broader base of benefactors.

Admittedly, it's more work to raise money when you're knocking on more doors. We'd all wish we could wave a magic wand and somehow all the big organizations would step forward and offer up unlimited resources. It's a nice dream. But the reality is that we think of our initial donations more like start-up funds—the absolutely essential resources that get the Foundation going, giving us the chance to reach a broader audience of people who share our commitment to and passion for supporting education.

Frankly, it's a lot of hard work. But it's a job that's got to be done. It's a job that, in a sense, will never be finished because new students keep arriving every year. But working together we believe we can really make a difference—first, to the students, but ultimately we can help shape the future of our nation and our world.

15

MENTORING PARTNERSHIP

THE WASHINGTON STATE MENTORING PARTNERSHIP (WSMP) was initiated in 1999 by the Department of Social and Health Services. The WSMP expanded in 2004 with the support of Costco Wholesale. Today, it is poised to help close the mentoring gap in Washington.

The mentoring gap refers to the number of young people in Washington who could benefit from a mentor but do not have one. Today, there are 1.5 million young people in our state under the age of 18. According to a recent WSMP survey, more than 240,000 of those folks could benefit from a mentoring relationship, yet only 20,000 have a mentor. The WSMP's mission is to eliminate this gap.

Mentoring is a structured and trusting relationship that brings young people together with caring individuals who offer guidance, support, and encouragement aimed at developing the competence and character of the student.

Traditional mentoring matches one adult with one young person; however, mentoring may take a variety of forms. For instance, group mentoring matches one adult with up to four young people. Peer mentoring matches a caring youth with other youth. E-mentoring is conducted via email.

As the case of e-mentoring suggests, mentoring can take place in a range of settings. Many school-based mentoring programs have their mentors and protégés meet on school grounds. Similarly, community-based mentoring programs may have matches meet at their offices. Some matches may meet at a juvenile correctional facility.

Typically, mentors and their protégés meet at least four hours a month for a year. There are, of course, exceptions to this rule. Many school-based programs coincide with the school year, matching mentors and protégés for a period of nine to ten months. While the length of individual meetings and the duration of the match may differ from program to program, it is important that both mentor and protégé establish expectations about such matters at the outset of a relationship.

The WSMP is advised by two bodies, our Leadership and Provider Councils. The latter group is comprised of 25 mentoring providers from across the state. The Provider Council is instrumental in helping the WSMP identify the needs of mentoring providers in Washington. The Provider Council is co-chaired by Pamela Dailey of Clark County Department of Human Services and Hazel Cameron of the 4Cs Mentoring Coalition.

The WSMP also receives support and direction from our Leadership Council. This body is made up of influential members of the private and public sector who help develop and maintain the WSMP's vision. The Leadership Council is co-chaired by Lieutenant Governor Brad Owen and WSU alumnus and legendary Cougar quarterback, Jack Thompson.

For more information on the Washington Mentoring Partnership, visit their website at *http://www.washingtonmentoring.org*

RECOMMENDATIONS
FROM THE 2020 COMMISSION *LEARNING FOR LIFE*

THE 15 RECOMMENDATIONS from the Report of the 2020 Commission on the Future of Post-Secondary Education:

1. Increase the capacity of the post-secondary education system so that by the year 2020, all Washington residents who want to learn will have access to the education or training appropriate to their aspirations and their level of knowledge.

2. Use all accredited post-secondary education providers to meet the expected surge in demand for post-secondary education.

3. Create a scholarship for all students who earn a Certificate of Mastery and graduate from high school. This scholarship should be sufficient to pay tuition for a minimum of two years of post-secondary education.

4. Expand and improve the information and counseling available to students and their families, so that they can make better choices about the post-secondary education options available to them.

5. Maintain the base funding of public institutions at or above the average of public per-student funding of peer institutions in other states.

6. Provide incentive funding above the base to public institutions that propose and achieve improvements in educational quality and/or reduce costs. This funding should be offered in the form of venture capital for institutional initiatives that accomplish specific state policy objectives.

7. Move toward assessing education in terms of what students learn rather than how many hours they spend in class.

8. Create incentives for educators to accelerate student progression through high school and post-secondary education when appropriate.

9. Designate a statewide coordinator who will make distance education easy to use.

10. Eliminate or amend laws, regulations, and practices that unreasonably restrict institutions' ability to operate efficiently.

11. Grant tuition-setting authority to the State Board for Community and Technical Colleges and to the governing boards of all four-year public post-secondary institutions.

12. Continue innovation and efficiency measures to mitigate the cost of increasing capacity and improving quality.

13. Make post-secondary education a higher priority in the state budget in order to create a system of sufficient size and quality to meet the needs of Washington residents. Provide the resources needed by considering all viable options, including a public referendum adjusting the state spending limit as that becomes necessary.

14. Clarify the division of labor for governing post-secondary education. Review the statutory responsibilities of the Higher Education Coordinating Board and eliminate non-essential functions so that it can focus on its central mission as the statewide planning agency. Strengthen the autonomy and responsibility of Boards of Regents and Trustees.

15. Establish an independent, non-profit organization to build and sustain public understanding of the need for higher levels of educational attainment and lifelong learning. This group should be both an independent advocate for post-secondary education, and an organization that urges the system to high standards of accessibility, quality, innovation, efficiency, and responsiveness to the needs of learners.

The entire report is available by visiting:

http://www.digitalarchives.wa.gov/governorlocke/taskcomm/2020/learning.htm#h

SEATTLE-BASED WRITER **TONY DIRKSEN** has held creative and management positions with Apple Computer, Microsoft Corporation, and Sunset Books. As founder and principal of Redmond Advisors, he has been responsible for producing strategic investor materials for companies such as Amazon.com and AT&T Corporation. He has also done extensive work for several nonprofit organizations including the Washington Education Foundation.

In 2005 Tony launched *Radio Whisky*, the first podcast dedicated to the world of spirits, and this year is launching *Radio Comet*, a children's fiction site.

Tony attended the University of California at Berkeley and did his graduate work in journalism at the University of Oregon.